greatest ever

Quick & easy

p

This is a Parragon Publishing Book
This edition published in 2004

Parragon Publishing
Queen Street House
4 Queen Street
Bath BA1 1HE, UK

ISBN: 1-40543-290-X

Printed in Indonesia

Produced by the Bridgewter Book Company Ltd.

NOTE

Cup measurements in this book are for American cups. This book also uses
imperial and metric measurements. Follow the same units of measurement
throughout; do not mix imperial and metric.
All spoon measurements are level: teaspoons are assumed to be 5 ml and
tablespoons are assumed to be 15 ml.Unless otherwise stated, milk is assumed
to be whole milk,eggs and individual vegetables such as potatoes are medium,
and pepper is freshly ground black pepper.

The times given for each recipe are an approximate guide only because the
preparation times may differ according to the techniques used by different
people and the cooking times may vary as a result of the type of oven used.

Recipes using raw or very lightly cooked eggs should be
avoided by infants, the elderly, pregnant women, convalescents, and anyone
suffering from an illness.

Contents

Introduction

This book is designed to appeal to anyone who
wants a wholesome but quick and easy diet, and
includes many recipes suitable for vegetarians
and vegans. Its main aim is to show people that,
with a little forethought, it is possible to spend
very little time in the kitchen while still enjoying

appetizing food. The recipes collected together come from all over the world;
some of the Asian and barbecue dishes featured require marinating, often
overnight, but it is worth remembering that their actual cooking time is very
short once the marinade has been absorbed.

The more exotic dishes on offer are balanced by some traditional dishes,
which are sure to become firm family favorites. If you want fast food for
everyday meals, or you are short on time and want to prepare a tasty dinner
party treat, there is something for everybody in this book. To save time in the
kitchen, always make sure that you have a stock of staple foodstuffs such as
rice, pasta, spices, and herbs, so that you can easily turn your hand to any
number of these recipes.

Flour

You will need to keep a selection of flour: Self-rising and whole-wheat are the most useful. You may also like to keep rice flour and cornstarch for thickening sauces and to add to cakes, and desserts.

Grains and Rice

A good variety of grains is essential. For rice, choose from long-grain, basmati, Italian risotto, short-grain, and wild rice. Other grains add variety to the diet. Try to include barley millet, bulgar wheat, polenta, oats, semolina, and tapioca.

Pasta

Pasta is very popular and there are many types and shapes to choose from. Keep a good selection, such as tagliatelle, fettuccine, and fusilli.

Herbs

A good selection of herbs is important for adding variety to your cooking. You should store dried basil, thyme, bay leaves, oregano, rosemary, mixed herbs, and bouquet garni.

Spices

Your basic stock of spices should include fresh chiles, ginger root and garlic, chili powder, turmeric, paprika, cloves, cardamom, black pepper, ground coriander, and ground cumin. The powdered spices will keep very well in airtight containers, while the fresh chile, ginger root and garlic will keep for 7–10 days in the refrigerator.

Legumes

Legumes are a valuable source of protein, vitamins, and minerals. Stock up on dried or canned soybeans, navy beans, red kidney beans, cannellini beans, garbanzo beans, lentils, split peas, and wax beans.

Dried Fruits

Currants, raisins, golden raisins, dates, apples, apricots, figs, pears, peaches, prunes, papayas, mangoes, figs, bananas, and pineapples can all be used in many different recipes.

Oils and Fats

Oils add subtle flavorings to foods, so it is a good idea to have a selection in your cupboard. Use a light olive oil for cooking and extra virgin olive oil for salad dressings. Use corn oil as a general-purpose oil. Sesame oil is wonderful in stir-fries; hazelnut and walnut oils are superb in salad dressings.

Vinegars

Choose three or four vinegars – red or white wine, cider, light malt, tarragon, sherry, or balsamic vinegar, to name just a few. Each will add its own character to your recipes.

Mustards

Mustards are made from black, brown, or white mustard seeds which are ground and mixed with spices. Meaux mustard has a grainy texture with a warm taste. Dijon mustard has a sharp flavor while American mustard is mild and sweet.

Basic Recipes

Fresh Chicken Bouillon

MAKES 7½ CUPS

2 lb 4 oz/1 kg chicken, skinned

2 celery stalks

1 onion

2 carrots

1 garlic clove

few fresh parsley sprigs

9 cups water

salt and pepper

1 Put all the ingredients into a large pan and bring to a boil over a medium heat.

2 Using a slotted spoon, skim away any scum on the surface. Reduce the heat to a gentle simmer, partially cover, and cook for 2 hours. Let cool.

3 Line a strainer with clean cheesecloth and put over a large pitcher or bowl. Pour the bouillon through the strainer. The cooked chicken can be used in another recipe. Discard the other solids. Cover the bouillon and chill in the refrigerator.

4 Skim away any fat that forms before using. Store in the refrigerator for 3–4 days, until required, or freeze in small batches.

Fresh Vegetable Bouillon

This can be kept chilled for up to 3 days or frozen for up to 3 months. Salt is not added when cooking the bouillon: it is better to season it according to the dish in which it is to be used.

MAKES 6¼ CUPS

9 oz/250 g shallots

1 large carrot, diced

1 celery stalk, chopped

½ fennel bulb

1 garlic clove

1 bay leaf

few fresh parsley and tarragon sprigs

8¾ cups water

pepper

1 Put all the ingredients into a large pan and bring to a boil over a medium heat.

2 Using a slotted spoon, skim away any scum on the surface. Reduce the heat to a gentle simmer, partially cover, and cook for 45 minutes. Let cool.

3 Line a strainer with clean cheesecloth and put over a large pitcher or bowl. Pour the bouillon through the strainer). Discard the herbs and vegetables.

4 Cover and store in small quantities in the refrigerator for up to 3 days.

Fresh Lamb Bouillon

MAKES 7½ CUPS

about 2 lb 4 oz/1 kg bones from
   a cooked joint or raw chopped
   lamb bones
2 onions, studded with 6 cloves, or
   sliced or chopped coarsely
2 carrots, sliced
1 leek, sliced
1–2 celery stalks, sliced
1 bouquet garni
about 2 quarts water

1 Chop or break up the bones and put into a large pan with the other ingredients.

2 Bring to a boil over a medium heat. Using a slotted spoon, skim away any scum on the surface. Reduce the heat, partially cover, and cook gently for 3–4 hours. Strain the bouillon and let cool.

3 Remove any fat from the surface and chill in the refrigerator. If stored for more than 24 hours the bouillon must be boiled every day, cooled quickly and chilled again. The bouillon may be frozen for up to 2 months; put into a large plastic bag and seal, leaving at least 1 inch/ 2.5 cm of headspace to allow for expansion.

Fresh Fish Bouillon

MAKES 7½ CUPS

1 head of a cod or salmon, etc. plus
   the trimmings, skin and bones or
   just the trimmings, skin and bones
1–2 onions, sliced
1 carrot, sliced
1–2 celery stalks, sliced
good squeeze of lemon juice
1 bouquet garni or 2 bay leaves

1 Wash the fish head and trimmings and put into a pan. Cover with water and bring to a boil over a medium heat.

2 Using a slotted spoon, skim away any scum on the surface, then add the remaining ingredients. Cover and simmer for 30 minutes.

3 Strain and let cool. Store in the refrigerator and use within 2 days.

Cornstarch Paste

Cornstarch paste is made by mixing 1 part cornstarch with about 1½ parts of cold water. Stir until smooth. The paste is used to thicken sauces.

Soups

The soups in this chapter combine a variety of flavors and textures from all over the world. There are thicker soups, thin clear consommés, and soups to appeal to vegetarians. The range of soups include thick and creamy winter warmers, and light and spicy Asian recipes. Many have been chosen because of their nutritional content and may be eaten as part of a low-fat diet. All, however, can be eaten as starters or as a light meal with fresh bread. The recipes are taken from all over the world, with special emphasis on Mediterranean, Indian, and Asian soups—something to please everybody.

artichoke soup

serves four

1 tbsp olive oil

1 onion, chopped

1 garlic clove, minced

1 lb/12 oz/ 800 g canned artichoke
hearts, drained

2½ cups hot vegetable bouillon

⅔ cup light cream

2 tbsp fresh thyme, stalks removed

2 sun-dried tomatoes, cut into strips

COOK'S TIP
Try adding 2 tbsp of dry
vermouth, such as Martini, to the
soup in step 5.

---

1 Heat the oil in a large pan over a medium heat. Add the onion and garlic, then cook until just softened.

2 Using a sharp knife, coarsely chop the artichoke hearts. Add the artichoke pieces to the onion and garlic mixture in the pan. Pour in the hot vegetable bouillon, stirring.

3 Bring the mixture to a boil over a medium heat, then reduce the heat, cover and simmer for 3 minutes.

4 Transfer the soup to a food processor or blender and process until smooth. Alternatively, push through a strainer to remove lumps.

5 Return the soup to the pan and stir in the cream and thyme.

6 Transfer the soup to a large bowl, cover and chill in the refrigerator for about 3–4 hours.

7 Ladle the chilled soup into 4 soup bowls and garnish with strips of sun-dried tomato. Serve immediately.

red bell pepper soup

serves four

8 oz/225 g red bell peppers, seeded
    and sliced

1 onion, sliced

2 garlic cloves, minced

1 fresh green chile, chopped

1¼ cups strained tomatoes

2½ cups vegetable bouillon

2 tbsp chopped fresh basil

fresh basil sprigs, to garnish

VARIATION

This soup is also delicious
served cold with ⅔ cup
plain yogurt swirled into it.

1 Put the red bell peppers in a large pan with the onion, garlic, and chili. Add the strained tomatoes and vegetable bouillon, then bring to a boil over a medium heat, stirring constantly.

2 Reduce the heat and simmer for 20 minutes, or until the peppers have softened. Drain and set aside the liquid and vegetables separately.

3 Puree the vegetables by pressing through a strainer with the back of a spoon. Alternatively, process in a food processor until smooth.

4 Return the vegetable puree to a clean pan and add the cooking liquid. Add the chopped basil and heat until hot. Ladle the soup into 4 bowls and garnish with basil sprigs. Serve.

mushroom noodle soup

serves four

4½ oz/125 g flat or open
    cup mushrooms
½ cucumber
2 scallions
1 garlic clove, peeled
2 tbsp vegetable oil
2½ cups water
1 oz/25 g Chinese rice noodles
¾ tsp salt
1 tbsp soy sauce

COOK'S TIP

Scooping the seeds out from the cucumber gives it a prettier effect when sliced, and also helps to reduce any bitterness, but if you prefer, you can leave them in.

1 Wash the mushrooms and pat them dry on paper towels. Slice thinly. Do not remove the mushroom peel as this adds more flavor.

2 Cut the cucumber in half lengthwise. Taking care not to damage the flesh, scoop out the seeds, using a teaspoon, then slice the cucumber thinly.

3 Chop the scallions finely and cut the garlic into thin strips.

4 Heat the oil in a large pan or wok over a medium heat.

5 Add the scallions and garlic to the pan or wok and cook for 30 seconds. Add the mushrooms and cook for an additional 2–3 minutes.

6 Stir in the water. Break the noodles into short lengths and add to the pan. Bring the soup to a boil over a medium heat, stirring occasionally.

7 Add the cucumber slices, salt, and soy sauce and simmer for about 2–3 minutes.

8 Ladle the mushroom noodle soup into 4 large, warmed soup bowls, distributing the noodles and vegetables evenly. Serve immediately.

mushroom & ginger soup

serves four

15 g/½ oz dried Chinese
mushrooms or 4½ oz/125 g field
or crimini mushrooms

4 cups hot vegetable bouillon

4½ oz/125 g egg thread noodles

2 tsp corn oil

3 garlic cloves, minced

1-inch/2.5-cm piece fresh
gingerroot, shredded finely

½ tsp mushroom catsup

1 tsp light soy sauce

4½ oz/125 g bean sprouts

fresh cilantro leaves, to garnish

COOK'S TIP

Rice noodles contain no fat
and are ideal for for anyone
on a lowfat diet.

1 Soak the dried mushrooms (if
using) for at least 30 minutes in
1¼ cups of the bouillon. Remove and
discard the stalks from the fresh
mushrooms, then slice. Drain the dried
mushrooms and set aside the bouillon.

2 Bring a large pan of water to a
boil over a medium heat. Add the
noodles and cook for 2–3 minutes.
Drain thoroughly and rinse. Set aside.

3 Heat a large wok over a high
heat. Add the oil and when hot,
add the garlic and ginger. Stir and add
the mushrooms. Stir for 2 minutes.

4 Add the remaining vegetable
bouillon with the reserved
bouillon and bring to a boil over a high
heat. Add the catsup and soy sauce.

5 Stir in the bean sprouts and cook
until tender. Put some noodles
into each bowl and ladle the soup on
top. Garnish with cilantro and serve.

lettuce & beancurd soup

serves four

7 oz/200 g beancurd,
    (drained weight)

2 tbsp vegetable oil

1 carrot, sliced thinly

½-inch/1-cm piece fresh gingerroot,
    cut into thin shreds

3 scallions, sliced diagonally

5 cups vegetable bouillon

2 tbsp soy sauce

2 tbsp dry sherry

1 tsp sugar

4½ oz/125 g romaine lettuce, shredded

salt and pepper

COOK'S TIP

For a pretty effect, score grooves
along the length of the carrot
with a sharp knife before slicing.
This will create a flower effect as
the carrot is cut into rounds.

1 Using a sharp knife, cut the
beancurd into small cubes.

2 Heat a large wok over a high
heat. Add the oil and when hot,
add the beancurd and cook until
browned. Remove with a slotted spoon
and drain on paper towels.

3 Add the carrot, ginger, and
scallions to the wok and cook for
2 minutes.

4 Add the vegetable bouillon, soy
sauce, sherry, and sugar to the
wok. Stir well to mix. Bring to a boil
over a medium heat and simmer for
1 minute. Add the romaine lettuce to
the wok and stir until it wilts.

5 Return the beancurd to the wok
to heat through. Season to taste
with salt and pepper and ladle into
4 warmed bowls and serve.

spicy dhal & carrot soup

serves six

⅔ cup split red lentils

5 cups vegetable bouillon

12 oz/350 g carrots, sliced

2 onions, chopped

8 oz/225 g canned
   chopped tomatoes

2 garlic cloves, chopped

2 tbsp ghee or vegetable oil

1 tsp ground cumin

1 tsp ground coriander

1 fresh green chile, seeded and
   chopped or 1 tsp minced chile

½ tsp ground turmeric

1 tbsp lemon juice

salt

1¼ cups milk

2 tbsp chopped fresh cilantro

unsweetened plain yogurt, to serve

COOK'S TIP

Lentils play an important part in ensuring that a healthy diet is maintained and provide energy-rich carbohydrates. Current guidelines recommend that 50% of our daily energy requirements come from carbohydrates.

1 Put the lentils into a strainer and rinse well under cold running water. Drain and put into a large pan, together with 2½ cups of the bouillon, the carrots, onions, tomatoes, and garlic. Bring the mixture to a boil over a medium heat, then cover and simmer for 30 minutes, or until the vegetables and lentils are tender.

2 Meanwhile, heat the ghee or oil in a small pan over a low heat. Add the cumin, ground coriander, chile, and turmeric and cook for 1 minute. Remove from the heat and stir in the lemon juice. Season with salt to taste.

3 Working in batches, transfer the soup to a blender and process until smooth. Return to the pan, add the spice mixture and the remaining 2½ cups of bouillon and cook over a low heat for 10 minutes.

4 Add the milk, taste, and adjust the seasoning, if necessary. Stir in the chopped cilantro and heat gently. Ladle the soup into 6 warmed bowls, and serve hot with a swirl of yogurt.

garbanzo bean soup

serves four

2 tbsp olive oil

2 leeks, sliced

2 zucchini, diced

2 garlic cloves, minced

1 lb 12 oz/800 g canned
    chopped tomatoes

1 tbsp tomato paste

1 bay leaf

3 cups vegetable bouillon

14 oz/400 g canned garbanzo
    beans, drained and rinsed

8 oz/225 g spinach

TO SERVE

freshly grated Parmesan cheese

sun-dried tomato bread

1 Heat the oil in a large pan over a medium heat. Add the leeks and zucchini and cook them for 5 minutes, stirring constantly.

2 Add the garlic, tomatoes, tomato paste, bay leaf, vegetable bouillon, and garbanzo beans.

3 Bring to a boil, then reduce the heat and simmer for 5 minutes.

4 Shred the spinach finely, add to the soup and cook for 2 minutes. Season to taste with salt and pepper.

5 Remove the bay leaf and discard. Ladle the soup into 4 bowls and serve with the Parmesan cheese and warmed sun-dried tomato bread.

COOK'S TIP

Garbanzo beans are used extensively in North African cuisine and are also found in Spanish and Asian cooking. They have a nutty flavor with a firm texture and are excellent canned.

tomato & pasta soup

serves four

4 tbsp unsalted butter

1 large onion, chopped

2½ cups vegetable bouillon

2 lb/900 g Italian plum tomatoes,
    peeled and chopped coarsely

pinch of baking soda

2 cups dried fusilli

1 tbsp superfine sugar

⅝ cup heavy cream

salt and pepper

fresh basil leaves, to garnish

1 Melt the butter in a large pan over a medium heat. Add the onion and cook for 3 minutes. Add 1¼ cups of vegetable bouillon to the pan, with the tomatoes, and baking soda. Bring to a boil, then reduce the heat and simmer for 20 minutes.

2 Remove the pan from the heat and let cool. Transfer the soup to a blender and process until smooth. Pour through a fine strainer back into the rinsed out pan.

3 Add the remaining vegetable bouillon and the pasta, and season to taste with salt and pepper.

4 Add the sugar to the pan and bring to a boil over a medium heat, then reduce the heat and simmer for about 15 minutes.

5 Ladle the soup into a warmed tureen, swirl the cream on top of the soup and garnish with fresh basil leaves. Serve immediately.

pumpkin soup

serves four

2 tbsp olive oil

2 medium onions, chopped

2 garlic cloves, chopped

2 lb/900 g pumpkin, peeled and cut
    into 1-inch/2.5-cm chunks

6¾ cups boiling vegetable or
    chicken bouillon

finely grated peel and juice of
    1 orange

3 tbsp fresh thyme leaves

⅔ cup milk

salt and pepper

crusty bread, to serve

COOK'S TIP

Pumpkins are usually
large vegetables. To make
things a little easier, ask the
grocer to cut a chunk off for you.
Alternatively, make double the
quantity and freeze the soup
for up to 3 months.

---

1 Heat the oil in a large pan over a medium heat. Add the onions and cook, stirring occasionally, for 3–4 minutes, or until softened. Add the garlic and pumpkin and cook, stirring, for an additional 2 minutes.

2 Add the boiling bouillon, orange peel and juice, and 2 tablespoons of the fresh thyme to the pan. Cover and simmer for 20 minutes, or until the pumpkin is tender.

3 Transfer to a blender and process until smooth. Alternatively, put the mixture into a bowl and mash with a potato masher until smooth. Season to taste with salt and pepper.

4 Return the soup to the pan and add the milk. Heat through for 3–4 minutes, or until piping hot, but not boiling.

5 Sprinkle with the remaining fresh thyme just before serving.

6 Ladle the soup into 4 warmed soup bowls and serve with lots of fresh crusty bread.

spinach & mascarpone soup

serves four

4 tbsp butter

1 bunch scallions, trimmed
  and chopped

2 celery stalks, chopped

12 oz/350 g spinach or sorrel
  or arugula

3 cups vegetable bouillon

8 oz/225 g mascarpone cheese

1 tbsp olive oil

2 slices thick-cut bread, cut
  into cubes

½ tsp caraway seeds

salt and pepper

sesame grissini, to serve

1 Melt half the butter in a very large pan over a medium heat. Add the scallions and celery, and cook, stirring frequently, for about 5 minutes, or until softened.

2 Pack the spinach, sorrel, or arugula into the pan. Add the bouillon and bring to a boil over a medium heat, then reduce the heat, cover, and cook for 15–20 minutes.

3 Transfer the soup to a blender or food processor and process until smooth. Alternatively, rub through a strainer with the back of a spoon. Return to the pan.

4 Add the mascarpone cheese to the soup and heat gently, stirring constantly, until smooth and blended. Season to taste with salt and pepper.

5 Heat the remaining butter with the oil in a skillet over a medium heat. Add the bread cubes and cook, turning frequently, until golden brown, adding the caraway seeds toward the end of cooking, so they do not burn.

6 Ladle the soup into 4 warmed bowls. Sprinkle with the croutons and serve with the sesame grissini.

beet & potato soup

serves six

1 onion, chopped

12 oz/350 g potatoes, diced

1 small cooking apple, peeled,
    cored, and grated

3 tbsp water

1 tsp cumin seeds

1 lb 2 oz/500 g cooked beet, peeled
    and diced

1 bay leaf

pinch of dried thyme

1 tsp lemon juice

2½ cups hot vegetable bouillon

4 tbsp sour cream

salt and pepper

fresh dill sprigs, to garnish

1 Put the onion, potatoes, apple, and water in a large bowl. Cover and cook on HIGH for 10 minutes.

2 Stir in the cumin seeds and cook on HIGH for 1 minute.

3 Stir in the beet, bay leaf, thyme, lemon juice, and bouillon. Cover and cook on HIGH for 12 minutes, stirring halfway through. Set aside, uncovered, for 5 minutes.

4 Remove the bay leaf and discard. Strain the vegetables and set aside the liquid in a pitcher.

5 Put the vegetables with a little of the reserved liquid in a blender and process until smooth.

6 Pour the vegetable puree into a clean bowl with the reserved liquid and mix well. Season to taste with salt and pepper. Cover and cook on HIGH for 4–5 minutes, or until piping hot.

7 Ladle the soup into 6 warmed bowls. Swirl 1 tablespoon of sour cream into each serving and garnish with a few fresh dill sprigs.

sweet & sour cabbage soup

serves four–six

½ cup golden raisins

½ cup orange juice

1 tbsp olive oil

1 large onion, chopped

9 oz/250 g cabbage, shredded

2 apples, peeled and diced

½ cup apple juice

14 oz/400 g canned
    peeled tomatoes

1 cup tomato or vegetable juice

3½ oz/100 g pineapple flesh,
    chopped finely

5 cups water

2 tsp wine vinegar

salt and pepper

fresh mint leaves, to garnish

COOK'S TIP

You can use green or white
cabbage to make this soup,
but red cabbage would require
a much longer cooking time.
Savoy cabbage has too
powerful a flavor.

1 Put the golden raisins into a
bowl, pour the orange juice over
them, and let soak for 15 minutes.

2 Heat the oil in a large pan over a
medium heat. Add the onion and
cook, stirring occasionally, for about
3–4 minutes, or until just soft. Add the
cabbage and cook for an additional
2 minutes, but do not let it brown.

3 Add the apples and apple juice,
cover, and cook for 5 minutes.
Stir in the tomatoes, tomato juice,
pineapple, and water. Season to taste
with salt and pepper and add the
vinegar. Add the golden raisins with
the orange juice. Bring to a boil over a
medium heat, reduce the heat, partially
cover, and cook for 1 hour, or until the
fruit and vegetables are tender.

4 Remove the pan from the heat
and let cool slightly. Working in
batches, transfer the soup to a blender
or food processor and process until
smooth. (If using a food processor,
strain off the cooking liquid and set
aside. Puree the solids with enough
cooking liquid to moisten them, then
mix with the remaining liquid.)

5 Return the soup to the pan and
simmer for about 10 minutes to
heat through. Ladle into warmed
bowls and garnish with fresh mint
leaves. Serve immediately.

fresh mushroom soup

serves four

3 tbsp butter

1 lb 9 oz/700 g mushrooms, sliced

1 onion, chopped finely

1 shallot, chopped finely

3 tbsp all-purpose flour

2–3 tbsp sherry or dry white wine

6 cups vegetable bouillon

⅔ cup light cream

2 tbsp chopped fresh parsley

fresh lemon juice, optional

salt and pepper

TO GARNISH

4 tbsp sour cream

4 fresh herb sprigs

1 Melt half the butter in a large skillet over a medium heat. Add the mushrooms and season with salt and pepper. Cook for 8 minutes, or until golden, stirring occasionally at first, then more often after they start to color. Remove from the heat.

2 Melt the remaining butter in a pan over a medium heat. Add the onion and shallot, and cook for 2–3 minutes, or until just softened. Stir in the flour and cook for 2 minutes. Add the wine and bouillon and stir.

3 Set aside about one-quarter of the mushrooms and add the remainder to the pan. Reduce the heat, cover, and cook for 20 minutes.

4 Let cool slightly, then working in batches, transfer the soup to a blender or food processor and process until smooth. (If using a food processor, strain off the cooking liquid and set aside. Puree the soup solids with enough cooking liquid to moisten them, then mix well with the remaining liquid.)

5 Return the soup to the pan and stir in the reserved mushrooms, the cream, and parsley. Cook for about 5 minutes to heat through, taste and

adjust the seasoning, adding a little lemon juice if you wish. Ladle the soup into 4 large, warmed bowls and garnish with sour cream and fresh herb sprigs. Serve immediately.

parsnip soup with ginger

serves six

2 tsp olive oil

1 large onion, chopped

1 large leek, sliced

1 lb 12 oz/800 g parsnips, sliced

2 carrots, sliced thinly

4 tbsp grated fresh gingerroot

2–3 garlic cloves, chopped finely

grated peel of ½ orange

6¼ cups water

1 cup orange juice

salt and pepper

TO GARNISH

snipped fresh chives

finely grated orange peel

VARIATION
You could make the soup using equal amounts (1 lb/450 g each) of carrots and parsnips.

1 Heat the oil in a large pan over a medium heat. Add the onion and leek and cook, stirring occasionally, for about 5 minutes, or until softened.

2 Add the parsnips, carrots, ginger, garlic, grated orange peel, water, and a pinch of salt. Reduce the heat, cover, and simmer, stirring occasionally, for about 40 minutes, or until the vegetables have softened.

3 Remove from the heat and let cool slightly, then working in batches, transfer the soup to a blender or food processor, and process until a smooth puree forms.

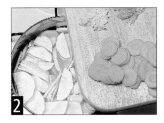

4 Return the soup to the pan and stir in the orange juice. Add a little water or more orange juice, if you prefer a thinner consistency. Season to taste with salt and pepper.

5 Simmer for about 10 minutes to heat through. Ladle the soup into 6 warmed bowls, garnish with chives and finely grated orange peel. Serve.

thick onion soup

serves four

6 tbsp butter

1 lb 2 oz/500 g onions,
    chopped finely

1 garlic clove, minced

⅓ cup all-purpose flour

2½ cups vegetable bouillon

2½ cups milk

2–3 tsp lemon or lime juice

good pinch of ground allspice

1 bay leaf

1 carrot, grated coarsely

4–6 tbsp heavy cream

2 tbsp chopped parsley

salt and pepper

CHEESE BISCUITS

½ cup whole-wheat flour

2 tsp baking powder

4 tbsp butter

4 tbsp freshly grated
    Parmesan cheese

1 egg, beaten

about 5 tbsp milk

1 Melt the butter in a pan over a low heat. Add the onions and garlic and cook, stirring frequently, for 10–15 minutes, or until softened, but not colored. Stir in the flour and cook, stirring, for 1 minute, then gradually stir in the bouillon and bring to a boil over a medium heat, stirring frequently. Add the milk, then bring back to a boil.

2 Season to taste with salt and pepper and add 2 teaspoons of the lemon juice, allspice, and bay leaf. Cover and simmer for 25 minutes, or until the vegetables are tender. Remove the bay leaf and discard.

3 Meanwhile, make the biscuits. Mix the flour, baking powder, and seasoning together. Rub in the butter until the mixture resembles fine bread crumbs, then stir in 3 tablespoons of the Parmesan cheese, the egg, and enough milk to mix to a soft dough.

4 Shape into a bar about ¾-inch/ 2-cm thick. Put onto a floured cookie sheet and mark into slices. Sprinkle with the remaining cheese and cook in a preheated oven at 425°F/220°C, for about 20 minutes, or until risen and golden brown.

5 Stir the carrot into the soup and simmer for 2–3 minutes. Add more lemon juice, if necessary. Stir in the cream and heat through. Garnish and serve with the biscuits.

gardener's broth

serves six

3 tbsp butter

1 onion, chopped

1–2 garlic cloves, minced

1 large leek

8 oz/225 g Brussels sprouts

4½ oz/125 g green beans

5 cups vegetable bouillon

1¼ cups frozen peas

1 tbsp lemon juice

½ tsp ground coriander

4 tbsp heavy cream

salt and pepper

MELBA TOAST

4–6 slices white bread

1 Melt the butter in a pan over a low heat. Add the onion and garlic and cook, stirring occasionally, until just soft, but not colored.

2 Slice the white part of the leek very thinly and set aside; slice the remaining leek. Slice the Brussels sprouts and thinly slice the beans.

3 Add the green part of the leeks, the Brussels sprouts, and beans to the pan. Add the bouillon and bring to a boil over a medium heat, then reduce the heat and simmer for 10 minutes.

4 Add the peas and seasoning. Add the lemon juice and cilantro, and continue to simmer for 10–15 minutes, or until the vegetables are tender.

5 Let cool slightly, then transfer the soup to a blender or food processor and process until smooth. Alternatively, rub through a strainer until smooth. Pour into a clean pan.

6 Add the reserved slices of leek, bring back to a boil, and simmer for about 5 minutes, or until the leek is tender. Adjust the seasoning, stir in the cream, and heat through gently.

7 To make the Melba toast, toast the bread on both sides under a preheated hot broiler. Cut horizontally through the slices, then toast the uncooked sides until they curl up. Serve immediately with the soup.

creamy onion & fava bean soup

serves five-six

1 tbsp butter

1 tsp oil

2 large onions, chopped finely

1 leek, sliced thinly

1 garlic clove, minced

5 cups water

6 tbsp white rice

1 bay leaf

½ tsp chopped fresh
    rosemary leaves

½ tsp chopped fresh thyme leaves

12 oz/350 g fresh or frozen fava
    beans, thawed if frozen

3½ oz/100 g rindless lean bacon,
    chopped finely

1½ cups milk, plus extra if needed

freshly grated nutmeg

salt and pepper

fresh herb sprigs, to garnish

1 Heat the butter and oil in a large pan over a medium heat. Add the onions, leek, and garlic. Season to taste with salt and pepper and cook for 10–15 minutes, stirring frequently, until the onion is soft.

2 Add the water, rice, and herbs with a large pinch of salt to the pan. Bring just to a boil over a medium heat, then reduce the heat to low. Cover and simmer for 15 minutes.

3 Add the fava beans, cover again and continue simmering for an additional 15 minutes, or until the vegetables are tender.

4 Remove the bay leaf and discard. let cool slightly, then, working in batches, transfer the soup to a blender or food processor and process until smooth. (If using a food processor, strain off the cooking liquid and set aside. Puree the solids with enough cooking liquid to moisten them, then mix with the remaining liquid.)

5 Put the bacon onto a large cookie sheet and put under a preheated hot broiler. Cook until crispy, turning the bacon over halfway through. Drain thoroughly on paper towels.

6 Return the soup to the pan and stir in the milk, adding extra, if you prefer a thinner consistency. Taste and adjust the seasoning, if necessary, then add a good grating of nutmeg. Cook over a low heat for 10 minutes, or until heated through, stirring occasionally. Ladle the soup into warmed bowls, sprinkle with bacon and garnish with herb sprigs. Serve.

chicken & pasta broth

serves six

12 oz/350 g boneless
    chicken breasts

2 tbsp corn oil

1 medium onion, diced

1½ cups carrots, diced

9 oz/250 g cauliflower flowerets

3¾ cups chicken bouillon

2 tsp dried mixed herbs

1¼ cups small pasta shapes

salt and pepper

freshly grated Parmesan
    cheese, optional

VARIATION

Broccoli flowerets can be used to replace the cauliflower flowerets. Substitute 2 tbsp of chopped fresh mixed herbs for the dried mixed herbs, if you wish.

1 Finely dice the chicken breasts with a sharp knife. Remove and discard any skin.

2 Heat the oil in a large heavy-bottomed pan or skillet over a medium-high heat. Add the diced chicken and the vegetables and quickly cook until they are lightly colored.

3 Stir in the bouillon and herbs. Bring to a boil and add the pasta shapes. Return to a boil, cover, and simmer for 10 minutes, stirring occasionally to prevent the pasta shapes sticking together.

4 Season to taste with salt and pepper, sprinkle with Parmesan cheese (if using) and serve.

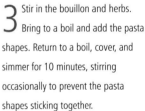

chicken & leek soup

serves six

12 oz/350 g boneless
   chicken breasts

12 oz/350 g leeks

2 tbsp butter

5 cups chicken bouillon

1 bouquet garni

8 pitted prunes

cooked rice and diced bell
   peppers, optional

salt and white pepper

VARIATION

Instead of the bouquet garni
sachet, you can use a bunch
of fresh, mixed herbs, tied
together with string. Choose
herbs such as parsley, thyme,
and rosemary.

---

1 Cut the chicken and leeks into
1-inch/2.5-cm pieces.

2 Melt the butter in a large pan
over a medium heat. Add the
chicken and leeks and cook for about
8 minutes, stirring occasionally.

3 Add the chicken bouillon and
bouquet garni to the mixture in
the pan, and season to taste with salt
and pepper.

4 Bring the soup to a boil over a
medium heat, then reduce the
heat and simmer for 45 minutes.

5 Add the pitted prunes with some
cooked rice and diced bell peppers
(if using), and simmer for 20 minutes.
Remove the bouquet garni and
discard. Ladle the soup into a warmed
tureen or individual bowls and serve.

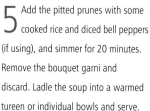

chunky potato & beef soup

serves four

2 tbsp vegetable oil

8 oz/225 g lean braising or frying
  steak, cut into strips

8 oz/225 g new potatoes, halved

1 carrot, diced

2 celery stalks, sliced

2 leeks, sliced

3¾ cups beef bouillon

8 baby corn cobs, sliced

1 bouquet garni

2 tbsp dry sherry

salt and pepper

chopped fresh parsley, to garnish

crusty bread, to serve

COOK'S TIP

Make double the quantity of
soup and freeze the remainder in
a rigid container for later use.
When ready to use, put in the
refrigerator to thaw thoroughly,
then heat until piping hot.

1 Heat the oil in a large pan over a medium heat. Add the strips of steak to the pan and cook for about 3 minutes, turning constantly.

2 Add the potatoes, carrot, and celery and leeks. Cook, stirring constantly, for an additional 5 minutes.

3 Pour in the beef bouillon and bring to a boil over a medium heat. Reduce the heat until the liquid is simmering gently, then add the sliced baby corn cobs and the bouquet garni.

4 Cook the soup for an additional 20 minutes, or until the meat and all the vegetables are tender.

5 Remove the bouquet garni from the pan and discard. Stir the dry sherry into the soup, then season to taste with salt and pepper.

6 Ladle the soup into 4 warmed soup bowls and garnish with the chopped fresh parsley. Serve with lots of crusty bread.

lamb & rice soup

serves four

5½ oz/150 g lean lamb

¼ cup rice

3¾ cups lamb bouillon

1 leek, sliced

1 garlic clove, sliced thinly

2 tsp light soy sauce

1 tsp rice wine vinegar

1 large open cap mushroom, sliced

salt

chopped fresh parsley, to garnish

1 Using a sharp knife, trim any fat from the lamb and cut the meat into thin strips. Set aside until required.

2 Bring a large pan of lightly salted water to a boil over a medium heat. Add the rice, bring back to a boil, stir once, reduce the heat and cook for 10–15 minutes, or until tender. Drain, rinse and drain again. Set aside.

3 Meanwhile, put the lamb bouillon into a large pan and bring to a boil over a medium heat.

4 Add the lamb strips, leek, garlic, soy sauce, and rice wine vinegar to the bouillon in the pan. Reduce the heat, then cover and simmer for about 10 minutes, or until the lamb is tender and cooked through.

5 Add the mushroom slices and the rice to the pan and cook for an additional 2–3 minutes, or until the mushroom is cooked through and the soup is piping hot.

6 Ladle the soup into 4 large, warmed soup bowls and garnish with chopped fresh parsley. Serve immediately.

bacon, bean & garlic soup

serves four

8 oz/225 g lean smoked back
　　bacon slices
1 carrot, sliced thinly
1 celery stalk, sliced thinly
1 onion, chopped
1 tbsp oil
3 garlic cloves, sliced
3 cups hot vegetable bouillon
7 oz/200 g canned
　　chopped tomatoes
1 tbsp chopped fresh thyme
about 14 oz/400 g canned
　　cannellini beans, drained
1 tbsp tomato paste
salt and pepper
freshly grated cheddar cheese,
　　to garnish

1 Chop 2 slices of the bacon and put into a bowl. Cook in the microwave on HIGH for 3–4 minutes, until the fat runs out and the bacon is well cooked. Stir the bacon halfway through cooking to separate the pieces. Transfer to a large plate lined with paper towels and let cool. When cool, the bacon pieces should be crisp and dry.

2 Put the carrot, celery, onion and oil into a large bowl. Cover and cook on HIGH for 4 minutes.

3 Chop the remaining bacon and add to the bowl with the garlic. Cover and cook on HIGH for 2 minutes.

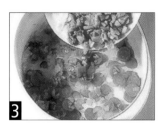

4 Add the bouillon, the chopped tomatoes, thyme, beans, and tomato paste. Cover and cook on HIGH for 8 minutes, stirring halfway through. Season to taste with salt and pepper. Ladle the soup into 4 warmed bowls and sprinkle with the crisp bacon and grated cheese. Serve immediately.

crab & ginger soup

serves four

1 carrot, chopped

1 leek, chopped

1 bay leaf

3¾ cups fish bouillon

2 medium-size cooked crabs

1-inch/2.5-cm piece fresh
    gingerroot, grated

1 tsp light soy sauce

½ tsp ground star anise

salt and pepper

COOK'S TIP

To prepare cooked crab, loosen
the meat from the shell by
banging the back of the
underside with a clenched fist.
Stand the crab on its edge with
the shell toward you. Force the
shell from the body with your
thumbs. Twist off the legs and
claws and remove the meat.
Twist off the tail and discard.
Remove and discard the gills
from each side of the body. Cut
the body in half along the center
and remove the meat. Scoop the
brown meat from the shell.

1 Put the carrot, leek, bay leaf, and bouillon into a large pan and bring to a boil over a medium heat. Reduce the heat, cover, and simmer for about 10 minutes, or until the vegetables are nearly tender.

2 Meanwhile, remove the meat from the cooked crabs. Break off the claws, break the joints, and remove the meat (you may require a fork for this). Add the crab meat to the fish bouillon in the pan.

3 Add the ginger, soy sauce, and star anise to the fish bouillon, then bring to a boil over a medium heat. Reduce the heat and simmer for 10 minutes, or until the vegetables are tender and the crab is heated through. Season to taste with salt and pepper.

4 Ladle the soup into 4 warmed serving bowls and garnish with crab claws. Serve immediately.

COOK'S TIP

If fresh crab meat is unavailable, use drained canned crab meat or thawed frozen crab meat.

clear chicken & egg soup

serves four

1 tsp salt

1 tbsp rice wine vinegar

4 eggs

3¾ cups chicken bouillon

1 leek, sliced

4½ oz/125 g broccoli flowerets

1 cup shredded cooked chicken

2 open cap mushrooms, sliced

1 tbsp dry sherry

dash of chilli sauce, or to taste

chilli powder, for sprinkling

VARIATION

You could use 4 dried
Chinese mushrooms, rehydrated
according to the package
instructions, instead
of the open cap mushrooms,
if you prefer.

---

1 Bring a large pan of water to a boil over a medium heat, Add the salt and rice wine vinegar.

2 Reduce the heat so it is just simmering and carefully break the eggs into the water, one at a time. Poach the eggs for 1 minute.

3 Remove the poached eggs with a slotted spoon and set aside.

4 Bring the bouillon to a boil in a separate pan over a medium heat. Add the leek, broccoli, chicken, mushrooms, and sherry. Add chilli sauce and cook for 10–15 minutes.

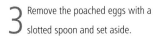

5 Add the poached eggs to the soup and cook for 2 minutes. Carefully Ladle the soup and poached eggs into 4 soup bowls. Sprinkle over a little chilli powder and serve.

shrimp soup

serves four

2 tbsp corn oil

2 scallions, thinly sliced diagonally

1 carrot, grated coarsely

125 g/4½ oz large closed cup
   mushrooms, sliced thinly

4 cups fish or vegetable bouillon

½ tsp Chinese five-spice powder

1 tbsp light soy sauce

125 g/4½ oz large, shelled shrimp
   or shelled jumbo shrimp, thawed
   if frozen

½ cup arugula, chopped coarsely

1 egg, well beaten

salt and pepper

4 large shrimp in shells, to
   garnish (optional)

1 Heat a wok over a medium heat and when hot, add the oil and swirl it around. Add the scallions and cook for 1 minute. Add the carrots and mushrooms, then cook for 2 minutes.

2 Add the bouillon and bring to a boil. Add the Chinese five-spice powder and soy sauce, and season to taste with salt and pepper. Simmer for 5 minutes.

3 If the shrimp are large, cut them in half before adding to the wok and simmer for 3–4 minutes.

4 Add the arugula and mix, then slowly pour in the beaten egg in a circular movement so it cooks in threads. Adjust the seasoning. Ladle the soup into 4 warmed bowls, top each with a whole shrimp and serve.

43

partan bree

serves six

1 medium-size boiled crab

scant ½ cup long-grain rice

2½ cups skim milk

2½ cups fish bouillon

1 tbsp anchovy paste

2 tsp lime or lemon juice

1 tbsp chopped fresh parsley or

   1 tsp chopped fresh thyme

3–4 tbsp sour cream, optional

salt and pepper

snipped fresh chives, to garnish

1 Remove all the brown and white meat from the cooked crab with a sharp knife and set aside until required. Carefully crack the claws, remove all the meat and chop coarsely. Set aside the claw meat.

2 Put the rice and milk into a pan and bring slowly to a boil over a medium heat. Cover and simmer gently for about 20 minutes.

3 Add the white and brown crab meat and season to taste with salt and pepper. Simmer for 5 minutes.

4 Let cool slightly, then transfer to a blender or food processor and process until smooth.

5 Pour the soup into a clean pan and add the fish bouillon and the claw meat. Bring slowly to a boil, then add the anchovy paste and lime juice. Adjust the seasoning.

6 Simmer for 2–3 minutes. Stir in the parsley. Ladle the soup into 6 bowls, swirl sour cream (if using) on the top, garnish with chives and serve.

smoked haddock soup

serves four

8 oz/225 g smoked haddock fillet

1 onion, chopped finely

1 garlic clove, minced

2½ cups water

2½ cups skim milk

2⅔–4 cups hot mashed potatoes

2 tbsp butter

about 1 tbsp lemon juice

6 tbsp lowfat plain yogurt

4 tbsp chopped fresh parsley

salt and pepper

1 Put the fish, onion, garlic, and water into a pan. Bring to a boil, cover, and simmer over a low heat for 15–20 minutes.

2 Remove the fish from the pan. Strip off the skin and remove all the bones, and set both aside. Flake the flesh finely with a fork.

3 Return the skin and bones to the cooking liquid and simmer for 10 minutes. Strain, discarding the skin and bones. Pour the cooking liquid into a clean pan.

4 Add the milk and flaked fish, then season to taste with salt and pepper. Bring to a boil and simmer for about 3 minutes.

5 Gradually whisk in enough mashed potato to give a fairly thick soup, then stir in the butter, and sharpen to taste with lemon juice.

6 Add the plain yogurt and 3 tablespoons of the chopped parsley. Heat through gently and adjust the seasoning, if necessary. Ladle the soup into 4 warmed bowls, sprinkle with the remaining parsley and serve.

curried chicken & corn soup

serves four

1 cup canned corn, drained

3¾ cups chicken bouillon

12 oz/350 g cooked, lean chicken,
   cut into strips

16 baby corn cobs

1 tsp Chinese curry powder

½-inch/1-cm piece fresh
   gingerroot, grated

3 tbsp light soy sauce

2 tbsp snipped fresh chives

COOK'S TIP

Prepare the soup up to
24 hours in advance without
adding the chicken. Let cool,
cover, and store in the
refrigerator. Add the chicken
and heat the soup through
thoroughly before serving.

1 Put the canned corn in a food
processor, with ⅔ cup of the
chicken bouillon and process until a
smooth puree forms.

2 Pass the corn puree through a
fine strainer, pressing with the
back of a spoon to remove any husks.

3 Pour the remaining chicken
bouillon into a large pan and add
the strips of cooked chicken. Stir in the
corn puree and mix well.

4 Add the baby corn cobs and bring
the soup to a boil over medium
heat. Cook for 10 minutes.

5 Add the Chinese curry powder,
grated ginger, and light soy sauce
and stir well. Cook the soup for an
additional 10–15 minutes.

6 Stir in the snipped chives, then
ladle the soup into 4 warmed
soup bowls. Serve immediately.

avocado & mint soup

serves six

3 tbsp butter

6 scallions, sliced

1 garlic clove, minced

2 tbsp all-purpose flour

2½ cups vegetable bouillon

2 ripe avocados

2–3 tsp lemon juice

pinch of grated lemon peel

⅔ cup milk

⅔ cup light cream

1–1½ tbsp chopped fresh mint

salt and pepper

6 fresh mint sprigs, to garnish

MINTED GARLIC BREAD

5 tbsp butter

1–2 tbsp chopped fresh mint

1–2 garlic cloves, minced

1 whole-wheat or white French
    bread stick

1 Melt the butter in a large pan over a low heat. Add the scallions and garlic to the pan and cook, stirring occasionally, for about 3 minutes, or until soft and translucent.

2 Stir in the flour and cook, stirring, for 1–2 minutes. Gradually stir in the bouillon, then bring to a boil over a medium heat. Simmer gently while preparing the avocados.

3 Peel the avocados, discard the pits, and chop. Add to the soup with the lemon juice and peel. Season with salt and pepper. Cover and cook for 10 minutes, or until tender.

4 Let cool slightly, then transfer the soup to a blender and process until smooth. Alternatively, press through a strainer with the back of a spoon. Pour into a bowl.

5 Stir in the milk and cream, adjust the seasoning, then stir in the mint. Cover and chill thoroughly.

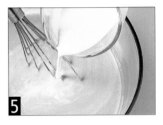

6 To make the minted garlic bread, soften the butter and beat in the mint and garlic. Cut the loaf into slanting slices, but leave a hinge on the bottom crust. Spread each slice with the butter and reassemble the loaf. Wrap in foil and put into a preheated oven, 350°F/180°C, for about 15 minutes.

7 Ladle the soup into 6 bowls and garnish with mint sprigs. Serve with the minted garlic bread.

Appetizers & Snacks

All of these recipes are easy to prepare and appetizing. They are colorful and flavorsome, providing an excellent beginning to any dinner party or just for an everyday snack. Depending on the main course, whet your guests' appetite with a tasty Eggplant Dipping Platter, Chinese Omelets, a Pâté, or delicious vegetable nibbles. Other quick and tasty snacks provide interesting colors and textures, and can all be rustled up at speed. In addition, all these quick recipes will satisfy your hunger pangs and tastebuds. All of these dishes are sure to get your meal off to the right start.

mint & cannellini bean dip

serves six

scant 1 cup dried cannellini beans
1 small garlic clove, minced
1 bunch of scallions,
    chopped coarsely
handful of fresh mint leaves·
2 tbsp sesame seed paste
2 tbsp olive oil
1 tsp ground cumin
1 tsp ground coriander
lemon juice
salt and pepper
fresh mint sprigs, to garnish
TO SERVE
fresh vegetable crudités, such as
    cauliflower flowerets, carrots,
    cucumber, radishes, and
    bell peppers

1 Put the cannellini beans into a bowl and pour over enough cold water to cover. Let soak for at least 4 hours, or overnight.

2 Drain the beans and rinse under cold running water. put them into a large pan, and cover with cold water. Bring to a boil over a high heat and boil rapidly for 10 minutes. Reduce the heat, cover, and simmer until tender.

3 Drain the beans thoroughly and transfer them to a food processor. Add the garlic, scallions, mint, sesame seed paste, and oil and process for 15 seconds. Alternatively, mash with a potato masher until smooth.

4 Scrape the mixture into a bowl, if necessary, and stir in the cumin, coriander, and lemon juice. Season to taste with salt and pepper. Mix thoroughly, cover with plastic wrap, and set aside in a cool place, but not the refrigerator, for 30 minutes to let the flavors develop.

5 Spoon the dip into small serving bowls and garnish with fresh mint sprigs. Put the bowls onto plates and surround them with vegetable crudités. Serve at room temperature.

tzatziki & black olive dips

serves four

½ cucumber

225 g/8 oz thick plain yogurt

1 tbsp chopped fresh mint

salt and pepper

4 pocket breads

DIP

2 garlic cloves, minced

⅔ cup pitted ripe black olives

4 tbsp olive oil

2 tbsp lemon juice

1 tbsp chopped fresh parsley

TO GARNISH

1 fresh mint sprig

1 fresh parsley sprig

1 To make the tzatziki, peel the cucumber and chop it coarsely. Sprinkle with salt and let stand for 15–20 minutes. Rinse under cold running water and drain thoroughly.

2 Mix the cucumber, yogurt, and mint together. Season to taste with salt and pepper and transfer to a serving bowl. Cover and chill in the refrigerator for 20–30 minutes.

3 To make the black olive dip, put the garlic and olives into a blender or food processor and process for 15–20 seconds. Alternatively, chop them very finely.

4 Add the oil, lemon juice, and parsley to the blender or food processor and process for a few more seconds. Alternatively, mix with the garlic and olives, and mash together. Season with salt and pepper.

5 Wrap the pocket breads in foil and either put over a barbecue grill for 2–3 minutes, turning once to warm through, or heat in a preheated oven or under a preheated broiler. Cut into pieces and serve with the tzatziki and black olive dips, garnished with fresh mint and parsley sprigs.

eggplant dipping platter

serves four

1 eggplant, peeled and cut into
   1-inch/2.5-cm cubes

3 tbsp sesame seeds, roasted in a
   dry pan over low heat

1 tsp sesame oil

grated peel and juice of ½ lime

1 small shallot, diced

1 tsp sugar

1 fresh red chile, seeded and sliced

4 oz/115 g broccoli flowerets

2 carrots, cut into batons

8 baby corn cobs, cut in
   half lengthwise

2 celery stalks, cut into batons

1 baby red cabbage, cut into
   8 wedges, the leaves of each
   wedge held together by the core

salt and pepper

VARIATION

You can vary the selection of
vegetables depending on your
preference or whatever you have
to hand. Other vegetables you
could use are cauliflower
flowerets and cucumber batons.

1 Bring a pan of water to a boil
over a medium heat. Add the
eggplant and cook for 7–8 minutes.
Drain thoroughly and let cool slightly.

2 Meanwhile, grind the sesame
seeds with the oil in a food
processor or in a mortar with a pestle.

3 Add the eggplant, lime peel and
juice, shallot, sugar, and chile to
the sesame seeds. Season to taste with
salt and pepper, then process until
smooth. Alternatively, chop and mash
by hand.

4 Adjust the seasoning to taste,
then spoon the dip into a bowl.

5 Serve the eggplant dipping platter
surrounded by the prepared
broccoli, carrots, baby corn, celery, and
red cabbage.

heavenly garlic dip

serves four

2 garlic bulbs

6 tbsp olive oil

1 small onion, chopped finely

2 tbsp lemon juice

3 tbsp sesame seed paste

2 tbsp chopped fresh parsley

salt and pepper

TO SERVE

fresh vegetable crudités

French bread or warmed
   pocket breads

VARIATION

If you come across smoked garlic, use it in this recipe—it tastes wonderful. There is no need to roast the smoked garlic, so omit the first step. This dip can also be used to baste vegetarian burgers.

1 Separate the garlic bulbs into individual cloves. Put them onto a large cookie sheet and roast in a preheated oven at 400°F/200°C, for about 8–10 minutes, then let cool for a few minutes.

2 When they are cool enough to handle, peel the garlic cloves and then chop them finely.

3 Heat the oil in a skillet over a low heat. Add the garlic and onion and cook, stirring occasionally, for 8–10 minutes, or until softened. Remove the pan from the heat.

4 Mix in the lemon juice, sesame seed paste, and chopped parsley. Season to taste with salt and pepper. Transfer the dip to a small bowl and keep warm while you prepare the vegetable crudites.

5 When ready to serve, garnish the dip with a parsley sprig and serve with vegetable crudités, with French bread or warm pocket breads.

mixed bean pâté

serves four

14 oz/400 g canned mixed
   beans, drained
2 tbsp olive oil
juice of 1 lemon
2 garlic cloves, minced
1 tbsp chopped fresh cilantro
2 scallions, chopped
salt and pepper
shredded scallions, to garnish

1 Rinse the mixed beans thoroughly under cold running water and drain well.

2 Transfer the beans to a food processor or blender and process until smooth. Alternatively, put the beans into a bowl and mash with a fork or potato masher.

3 Add the oil, lemon juice, garlic, cilantro, and scallions and blend until fairly smooth. Season to taste with salt and pepper.

4 Transfer the pâté to a serving bowl, cover, and chill in the refrigerator for at least 30 minutes.

5 Garnish the pâté with shredded scallions and serve.

lentil pâté

serves four

1 tbsp vegetable oil, plus extra
for oiling

1 onion, chopped

2 garlic cloves, minced

1 tsp garam masala

½ tsp ground coriander

3 cups vegetable bouillon

1 cup red split lentils

1 small egg

2 tbsp milk

2 tbsp mango chutney

2 tbsp chopped fresh parsley

chopped fresh parsley, to garnish

TO SERVE

salad greens

warm toast

VARIATION

Use other spices, such as chili
powder or Chinese five-spice
powder, to flavor the pâté,
and add tomato relish or chili
relish instead of the mango
chutney, if you prefer.

1 Heat the oil in a large pan over a medium heat. Add the onion and garlic and cook for 2–3 minutes, stirring. Add the spices and cook for an additional 30 seconds. Stir in the vegetable bouillon and lentils, and bring the mixture to a boil. Reduce the heat and simmer for 20 minutes, or until the lentils are cooked and soft. Remove the pan from the heat and drain off any excess moisture.

2 Transfer the mixture to a food processor and add the egg, milk, mango chutney, and chopped parsley. Blend until smooth.

3 Oil and line the bottom of a 1 lb/450 g loaf pan. Spoon the mixture into the pan, cover and cook in a preheated oven at 400°F/200°C, for 40–45 minutes, or until firm.

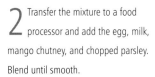

4 Let the pâté cool in the pan for 20 minutes, then transfer to the refrigerator to cool completely. Turn out onto a serving plate, garnish with parsley sprigs and serve in slices with salad greens and warm toast.

smoked fish & potato pâté

serves four

1 lb 7 oz/650 g mealy potatoes,
    peeled and diced

10½ oz/300 g smoked mackerel,
    skinned and flaked

3 oz/85 g cooked gooseberries

2 tsp lemon juice

2 tbsp low-fat sour cream

1 tbsp capers, rinsed

1 gherkin, chopped

1 tbsp chopped dill pickle

1 tbsp chopped fresh dill

salt and pepper

lemon wedges, to garnish

toast or warm crusty bread, to serve

COOK'S TIP

Use stewed, canned, or bottled
cooked gooseberries for
convenience and to save time,
or when fresh gooseberries
are out of season.

1 Bring a large pan of water to a boil over a medium heat. Add the potatoes and cook for 10 minutes, or until tender. Drain thoroughly.

2 Put the cooked potatoes into a food processor or blender. Add the skinned and flaked smoked mackerel and process for 30 seconds until fairly smooth. Alternatively, put the ingredients into a large bowl and mash with a fork.

3 Add the cooked gooseberries, lemon juice, and sour cream to the fish and potato mixture. Blend for an additional 10 seconds or mash well.

4 Stir in the capers, gherkin, dill pickle, and fresh dill. Season to taste with salt and pepper.

5 Turn the fish pâté into a serving dish and garnish with lemon wedges. Serve with slices of toast or warm bread cut into chunks or slices.

walnut, egg & cheese pâté

serves two

1 celery stalk

1–2 scallions

¼ cup shelled walnuts

1 tbsp chopped fresh parsley

1 tsp chopped fresh dill or

½ tsp dried dill

1 garlic clove, minced

dash of Worcestershire sauce

½ cup cottage cheese

2 oz/55 g blue cheese

1 hard-cooked egg

2 tbsp butter

salt and pepper

fresh herbs, to garnish

crackers, toast, or crusty bread,

to serve

3 Grate the blue cheese finely into the pâté mixture. Finely chop the hard-cooked egg and stir it into the mixture. Season to taste with salt and pepper.

1 Finely chop the celery, slice the scallions very thinly, and chop the walnuts evenly. Put into a bowl.

2 Add the chopped herbs, garlic and Worcestershire sauce to taste and mix well. Stir in the cottage cheese into the mixture and blend thoroughly.

4 Melt the butter in a small pan over a low heat, then stir it into the pate. Spoon into a serving dish or 2 individual dishes. Smooth the top, but do not press down firmly. Chill in the refrigerator until set.

5 Garnish with mixed herbs and serve with crackers, toast, or fresh crusty bread.

cheese, garlic & herb pâté

serves four

1 tbsp butter

1 garlic clove, minced

3 scallions, chopped finely

⅝ cup full-fat soft cheese

2 tbsp chopped mixed fresh herbs,
   such as parsley, chives,
   marjoram, oregano, and basil

1½ cups finely grated sharp
   cheddar cheese

pepper

4–6 slices of white bread from a
   medium-cut sliced loaf

TO GARNISH

ground paprika

1 fresh Italian parsley sprigs

TO SERVE

mixed salad greens

cherry tomatoes

1 Melt the butter in a small skillet over a low heat. Add the garlic and scallions and cook gently for 3–4 minutes, or until soft. Let cool.

2 Beat the soft cheese in a large mixing bowl until smooth, then add the garlic and scallions. Stir in the chopped mixed herbs and mix well.

3 Add the cheddar cheese and work the mixture together to form a stiff paste. Cover and chill in the refrigerator until ready to serve.

4 Toast the slices of bread on both sides, then cut off the crusts. Using a sharp bread knife, cut through the slices horizontally to make very thin slices. Cut into triangles, then lightly toast the untoasted sides under a preheated hot broiler until golden.

5 Arrange the mixed salad greens on 4 serving plates with the cherry tomatoes. Pile the cheese pâté on top and sprinkle with a little paprika. Garnish with a parsley sprig and serve with the toast.

crostini alla fiorentina

serves four

3 tbsp olive oil

1 onion, chopped

1 celery stalk, chopped

1 carrot, chopped

1–2 garlic cloves, minced

125 g/4½ oz chicken livers

4½ oz/125 g calf's, lamb's or
   pig's liver

⅔ cup red wine

1 tbsp tomato paste

2 tbsp chopped fresh parsley

3–4 canned anchovy fillets,
   chopped finely

2 tbsp bouillon or water

2–3 tbsp butter

1 tbsp capers

salt and pepper

chopped fresh parsley, to garnish

toasted bread, to serve

1 Heat the oil in a skillet over a low heat. Add the onion, celery, carrot, and garlic. Cook gently for 4–5 minutes, or until the onion is soft.

2 Meanwhile, rinse the chicken livers and pat dry on paper towels. Rinse the calf's or other liver and pat dry. Slice into strips. Add the liver to the skillet and cook gently for a few minutes, or until the strips are well sealed on all sides.

3 Add half the wine and cook until it has mostly evaporated. Add the rest of the wine, tomato paste, half the parsley, anchovies, bouillon or water, a little salt and plenty of pepper.

4 Cover the pan and simmer, stirring occasionally, for about 15–20 minutes, or until tender and most of the liquid has been absorbed.

5 Let the mixture cool slightly, then either coarsely mince or put into a food processor and process to a chunky puree.

6 Return to the pan and add the butter, capers, and remaining parsley. Heat through gently until the butter melts. Adjust the seasoning, if necessary. Spoon into a bowl and sprinkle with chopped parsley. Serve warm or cold spread on slices of toasted bread.

hummus & garlic toasts

serves four

14 oz/400 g canned garbanzo beans

juice of 1 large lemon

6 tbsp sesame seed paste

2 tbsp olive oil

2 garlic cloves, chopped finely

salt and pepper

GARLIC TOASTS

1 ciabatta loaf, sliced

2 garlic cloves, chopped finely

1 tbsp chopped fresh cilantro

4 tbsp olive oil

TO GARNISH

1 tbsp chopped fresh cilantro

pitted ripe black olives

1 To make the hummus, firstly drain the garbanzo beans and set aside a little of the liquid. Put the garbanzo beans and liquid into a food processor and blend, gradually adding the reserved liquid and lemon juice. Blend well after each addition until smooth.

2 Stir in the sesame seed paste and all but 1 teaspoon of the oil. Add the garlic, season to taste with salt and pepper, and blend again until smooth.

3 Spoon the hummus into a dish. Drizzle the remaining oil over the top and chill in the refrigerator.

4 To make the garlic toasts. Lay the slices of ciabatta on a broiler rack in a single layer.

5 Mix the garlic, cilantro, and oil together and drizzle over the bread slices. Cook under a preheated medium-hot broiler for 2–3 minutes until golden, turning once. To serve, garnish the hummus with cilantro and olives, then serve with the toasts..

pork sesame toasts

serves four

9 oz/250 g lean pork

⅔ cup raw shrimp, shelled
  and deveined

4 scallions, trimmed

1 garlic clove, minced

1 tbsp chopped fresh cilantro leaves
  and stems

1 tbsp fish sauce

1 egg

8–10 slices of thick-cut white bread

3 tbsp sesame seeds

⅔ cup vegetable oil

salt and pepper

TO GARNISH

fresh cilantro sprigs

½ red bell pepper, sliced finely

1 Put the pork, shrimp, scallions, garlic, cilantro, fish sauce, and egg into a food processor or blender. Season with salt and pepper and process for a few seconds until the ingredients are finely chopped. Transfer the mixture to a bowl. Alternatively, chop the pork, shrimp, and scallions very finely, and mix with the garlic, cilantro, fish sauce, and beaten egg. Season with salt and pepper and mix until well blended.

2 Spread the pork and shrimp mixture thickly over the slices of bread, so it reaches right up to the edges. Cut off the crusts and slice the bread into 4 squares or triangles.

3 Sprinkle the topping liberally with sesame seeds.

4 Heat a large wok over a medium heat. Add the oil and when hot, cook a few pieces of the bread, topping side down first so it sets the egg, for 2 minutes, or until golden brown. Turn the pieces over to cook on the other side, about 1 minute.

5 Drain the pork and shrimp toasts and drain on paper towels. Cook the remaining pieces. Arrange the toasts on a serving plate and garnish with fresh cilantro sprigs and strips of red bell pepper. Serve.

bruschetta with tomatoes

serves four

10½ oz/300 g cherry tomatoes

4 sun-dried tomatoes

4 tbsp extra virgin olive oil

16 fresh basil leaves, shredded

8 slices of ciabatta bread

2 garlic cloves, peeled

salt and pepper

VARIATION

Plum tomatoes are also good
in this recipe. Halve them, then
cut them into wedges. Mix
them with the sun-dried
tomatoes in step 3.

COOK'S TIP

Ciabatta is an Italian rustic
bread, which is slightly holey
and quite chewy. It is good
in this recipe, as it absorbs the
full flavor of the garlic and
extra virgin olive oil.

1 Using a sharp knife, cut the cherry tomatoes in half.

2 Using a sharp knife, slice the sun-dried tomatoes into strips.

3 Put the cherry tomatoes and sun-dried tomatoes into a small bowl. Add the oil and shredded basil leaves and toss to mix well. Season to taste with salt and pepper.

4 Lightly toast the ciabatta slices inder a preheated medium-hot broiler. Cut the garlic cloves in half.

5 Rub the garlic, cut-side down, over both sides of the toasted ciabatta slices.

6 Put the ciabatta slices onto a serving plate or individual plates and top with the tomato mixture. Serve.

pepper salad

serves four

1 onion

2 red bell peppers

2 yellow bell peppers

3 tbsp olive oil

2 large zucchini, sliced

2 garlic cloves, sliced

1 tbsp balsamic vinegar

1¾ oz/50 g canned anchovy
   fillets, chopped

¼ cup pitted ripe black
   olives, halved

1 tbsp chopped fresh basil

salt and pepper

TOMATO TOASTS

small French bread stick

1 garlic clove, minced

1 tomato, peeled and chopped

2 tbsp olive oil

1 Cut the onion into wedges. Core and seed the bell peppers, then cut into thick slices.

2 Heat the oil in a large heavy-bottomed skillet. Add the onion, bell peppers, zucchini, and garlic, and cook gently for about 20 minutes, stirring occasionally.

3 Add the vinegar, anchovies, and olives. Season to taste with salt and pepper. Mix and let cool.

4 To make the tomato toasts, cut the French bread diagonally into ½-inch/1-cm slices.

5 Mix the garlic, tomato, and oil together. Season to taste and spread thinly over each slice of bread.

6 Put the bread onto a cookie sheet, drizzle with the oil and cook in a preheated oven at 425°F/220°C, for 5–10 minutes, or until crisp. Spoon the salad onto 4 serving plates, garnish with a basil sprig, and serve with the tomato toasts.

onions à la grecque

serves four

1 lb/450 g shallots

3 tbsp olive oil

3 tbsp honey

1 garlic clove, chopped

2 tbsp white wine vinegar

3 tbsp dry white wine

1 tbsp tomato paste

2 celery stalks, sliced

2 tomatoes, seeded and chopped

salt and pepper

chopped celery leaves, to garnish

1 Peel the shallots. Heat the oil in a large heavy-bottomed pan over a high heat. Add the shallots and cook, stirring, for 3–5 minutes, or until they start to brown.

2 Add the honey and garlic, and cook for an additional 30 seconds, then add the vinegar and dry white wine, stirring well.

3 Stir in the tomato paste, celery, and tomatoes and bring to a boil over a high heat. Cook for about 5–6 minutes. Season to taste with salt and pepper and let cool slightly.

4 Spoon into a large serving dish, garnish with chopped celery leaves and serve warm or cold.

VARIATION
Use button mushrooms instead of the shallots and fennel instead of the celery for another great appetizer.

shrimp parcels

serves four

1 tbsp corn oil

1 red bell pepper, seeded and
   sliced thinly

¾ cup bean sprouts

finely grated peel and juice of 1 lime

1 fresh red chili, seeded and very
   finely chopped

1 tsp freshly grated fresh gingerroot

8 oz/225 g shelled shrimp

1 tbsp fish sauce

½ tsp arrowroot

2 tbsp chopped fresh cilantro

8 sheets phyllo pastry

2 tbsp butter

2 tsp sesame oil

3 tbsp vegetable oil

chili dipping sauce, to serve

COOK'S TIP

If using cooked shrimp, cook for
1 minute only, otherwise the
shrimp will toughen.

---

1 Heat a large wok over a high heat. Add the oil and when hot, add the red bell pepper and bean sprouts. Cook for 2 minutes, or until the vegetables have softened.

2 Remove the wok from the heat and toss in the lime peel and juice, red chile, ginger, and shrimp, stirring well.

3 Mix the fish sauce with the arrowroot and stir the mixture into the wok juices. Return the wok to the heat and cook, stirring, for 2 minutes, or until the juices thicken. Toss in the cilantro and mix well.

4 Lay the sheets of phyllo pastry out on a board. Melt the butter and sesame oil over a low heat and brush each pastry sheet with the mixture.

5 Spoon a little of the shrimp filling onto the top of each sheet, fold over each end, and carefully roll up to enclose the filling.

6 Heat a large wok over a medium heat. Add the oil and when hot, add the parcels, in batches. Cook for 2–3 minutes, or until crisp and golden. Put onto a serving plate and serve immediately with a chili dipping sauce.

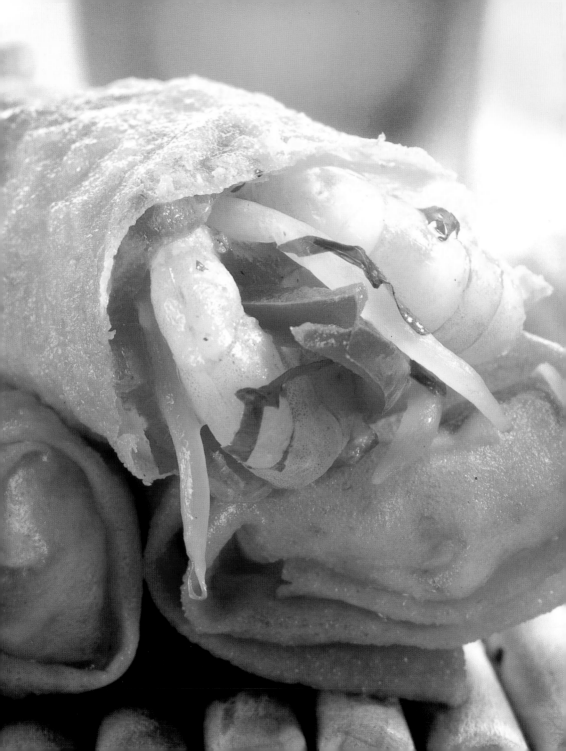

mussels in white wine

serves four

12 cups fresh mussels

¼ cup butter

1 large onion, chopped very finely

2–3 garlic cloves, minced

1½ cups dry white wine

⅔ cup water

2 tbsp lemon juice

good pinch of finely grated
    lemon peel

1 bouquet garni

1 tbsp all-purpose flour

4 tbsp light or thick cream

2–3 tbsp chopped fresh parsley

salt and pepper

crusty bread, to serve

1 Pull off all the "beards" from the mussels and scrub them under cold running water for 5 minutes to remove any mud, sand, and barnacles. Discard any mussels that refuse to close when tapped with a knife.

2 Melt half the butter in a large pan over a low heat. Add the onion and garlic, and cook gently until softened but not colored.

3 Add the wine, water, lemon juice and peel, and bouquet garni. Season to taste. Bring to a boil, then cover and simmer for 4–5 minutes.

4 Add the mussels to the pan, cover tightly and simmer for 5 minutes, shaking the pan frequently, until all the mussels have opened. Discard any mussels that have not opened. Remove the bouquet garni and discard.

5 Remove the empty half shell from each mussel. Blend the remaining butter with the flour and whisk into the liquid, a little at a time. Simmer for 2–3 minutes, or until thickened.

6 Add the cream and half the parsley and heat gently, then adjust the seasoning. Ladle the mussels and liquid into 4 large, warmed soup bowls, sprinkle with the remaining parsley and serve with plenty of warm crusty bread.

baked fennel

serves four

2 fennel bulbs

2 celery stalks, cut into 3-inch/
　7.5-cm pieces

6 sun-dried tomatoes, halved

scant 1 cup strained tomatoes

2 tsp dried oregano

⅔ cup freshly grated
　Parmesan cheese

1 Using a sharp knife, trim the fennel and discard any of the tough outer leaves and feathery fronds. Cut the bulb into fourths.

2 Bring a pan of water to a boil over a medium heat. Add the fennel and celery and cook until just tender. Remove and drain.

3 Put the fennel pieces, celery, and sun-dried tomatoes into a large ovenproof dish.

4 Mix the tomatoes and oregano together and pour the mixture over the fennel.

5 Sprinkle the top with the Parmesan cheese and cook in a preheated oven at 375°F/190°C, for 20 minutes, or until hot. Serve.

figs & prosciutto

serves four

1 cup arugula

4 fresh figs

4 slices prosciutto

4 tbsp olive oil

1 tbsp fresh orange juice

1 tbsp honey

1 small fresh red chile

COOK'S TIP

Chiles can burn the skin for several hours after chopping, so it is advisable to wear gloves when you are handling the very hot varieties.

1 Tear the arugula into more manageable pieces and arrange on 4 large serving plates.

2 Using a sharp knife, cut each of the figs into fourths and put them on top of the arugula.

3 Using a sharp knife, cut the prosciutto into strips and sprinkle over the arugula and figs.

4 Put the oil, orange juice, and honey in a screw-top jar and shake until the mixture emulsifies and forms a thick dressing. Transfer to a small bowl.

5 Using a sharp knife, dice the chile, remembering not to touch your face before you have washed your hands (see Cook's Tip). Add the chile to the dressing and mix well.

6 Drizzle the dressing over the prosciutto, arugula, and figs, tossing to mix well. Serve immediately.

capri salad

serves four

2 beefsteak tomatoes

4½ oz/125 g mozzarella cheese

12 ripe black olives

8 fresh basil leaves

1 tbsp balsamic vinegar

1 tbsp extra virgin olive oil

salt and pepper

fresh basil leaves, to garnish

COOK'S TIP

Buffalo mozzarella cheese, although it is usually more expensive because of the comparative rarity of buffalo, does have a better flavor than the cow's milk variety. It is popular in salads, but also provides a tangy layer in cooked dishes.

1 Using a sharp knife, cut the tomatoes into thin slices.

2 Drain the mozzarella cheese, if necessary, and cut into slices with a sharp knife.

3 Pit the black olives, if necessary and slice them into rings.

4 Layer the tomatoes, mozzarella slices, olives, and basil in a stack, finishing with a layer of cheese on top.

5 Put each stack under a preheated hot broiler and cook for about 2–3 minutes, or just long enough to melt the mozzarella.

6 Drizzle over the balsamic vinegar and oil, and season to taste with a little salt and pepper.

7 Transfer to 4 large serving plates and garnish with fresh a few basil leaves. Serve immediately.

cured meats, olives & tomatoes

serves four

4 plum tomatoes

1 tbsp balsamic vinegar

salt and pepper

6 canned anchovy fillets, drained
   and rinsed

¾ cup pitted green olives

2 tbsp capers, drained and rinsed

6 oz/175 g mixed, cured
   meats, sliced

8 fresh basil leaves

1 tbsp extra virgin olive oil

crusty bread, to serve

1 Using a sharp knife, cut the tomatoes into even-size slices. Sprinkle the tomato slices with the balsamic vinegar and season to taste with a little salt and pepper. Set aside.

2 Chop the anchovy fillets into pieces measuring about the same length as the olives.

3 Push a piece of anchovy and a caper into each olive.

4 Arrange the sliced meat onto 4 large serving plates, together with the tomatoes, filled olives, and basil leaves.

5 Lightly drizzle the oil over the sliced meat, tomatoes, and olives.

6 Serve the sliced meats, olives, and tomatoes with lots of fresh crusty bread.

stir-fried beancurd with chili sauce

serves four

1 lb 2 oz/500 g marinated or plain
firm beancurd (drained weight)

2 tbsp rice vinegar

2 tbsp sugar

1 tsp salt

3 tbsp smooth peanut butter

½ tsp chili flakes

3 tbsp barbecue sauce

4 cups corn oil

2 tbsp sesame oil

BATTER

4 tbsp all-purpose flour

2 eggs, beaten

4 tbsp milk

½ tsp baking powder

½ tsp chili powder

1 Cut the beancurd into 1-inch/
2.5-cm chunks, then set aside.

2 Mix the rice vinegar, sugar, and salt together in a pan. Bring to a boil over a low heat, then simmer for 2 minutes.

3 Remove the sauce from the heat and add the peanut butter, chili flakes, and barbecue sauce, stirring well until blended thoroughly.

4 To make the batter, sift the flour into a bowl, make a well in the center, and add the eggs. Draw in the flour, adding the milk slowly. Stir in the baking powder and chili powder.

5 Heat the corn oil and sesame oil together in a deep-fryer or large pan until a light haze appears on top.

6 Dip the beancurd chunks into the batter and deep-fry until golden brown, working in batches, if necessary. Drain on paper towels.

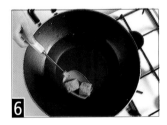

7 Transfer the beancurd chunks to a warmed serving dish and serve immediately with the peanut sauce.

spicy salt & pepper shrimp

serves four

9–10½ oz/250–300 g raw shrimp
   in their shells, thawed if frozen

1 tbsp light soy sauce

1 tsp Chinese rice wine or dry sherry

2 tsp cornstarch

1¼ cups oil for deep-frying

2–3 scallions, to garnish

SPICY SALT AND PEPPER

1 tbsp salt

1 tsp ground Szechuan peppercorns

1 tsp Chinese five-spice powder

1 Pull the soft legs off the shrimp, but keep the body shell on. Dry well on paper towels.

2 Put the shrimp into a large bowl with the soy sauce, Chinese rice wine or sherry, and cornstarch. Coat the shrimp thoroughly in the mixture and let marinate in the refrigerator for about 25–30 minutes.

3 To make the spicy salt and pepper, mix the salt, ground Szechuan peppercorns, and the Chinese five-spice powder together in a small bowl. Put the spicy salt and pepper mixture into a dry skillet and cook for about 3–4 minutes over a low heat, stirring constantly to prevent the spices burning on the bottom of the pan. Remove from the heat and let cool.

4 Heat a large wok over a high heat. Add the oil and when smoking, add the shrimp, in batches, and cook until golden brown. Remove the shrimp from the wok with a slotted spoon and drain on paper towels.

5 Put the scallions into a bowl, pour on 1 tablespoon of the hot oil and let stand for 30 seconds. Transfer the shrimp to a large serving plate and garnish with the scallions. Serve with the spicy salt and pepper as a dip.

deep-fried seafood

serves four

7 oz/200 g prepared squid

7 oz/200 g raw jumbo
  shrimp, shelled

5½ oz/150 g whitebait

1¼ cups oil for deep-frying

⅓ cup all-purpose flour

1 tsp dried basil

salt and pepper

Garlic Mayonnaise, to serve
  (see Cook's Tip)

COOK'S TIP

To make the Garlic Mayonnaise,
mince 2 garlic cloves, stir into
8 tbsp of mayonnaise, then
season to taste with salt and
pepper and a little chopped fresh
parsley. Cover with plastic wrap
and chill in the refrigerator.

1 Carefully rinse the squid, shrimp, and whitebait under cold running water, completely removing any dirt or grit.

2 Using a sharp knife, slice the squid into thin rings, leaving the tentacles whole.

3 Heat the oil in a large pan to 350°–375°F/180°–190°C, or until a cube of bread browns in 30 seconds.

4 Put the flour into a large bowl and season with the salt, pepper, and dried basil.

5 Roll the squid, shrimp, and whitebait in the seasoned flour until coated thoroughly all over. Carefully shake off any excess flour.

6 Cook the seafood, in batches, in the hot oil for 2–3 minutes, or until crispy and golden all over. Remove the seafood with a slotted spoon and let drain thoroughly on paper towels.

7 Transfer the deep-fried seafood to 4 large serving plates and serve with Garlic Mayonnaise (see Cook's Tip).

chinese omelet

serves four

8 eggs

8 oz/225 g cooked
   chicken, shredded

12 raw jumbo shrimp, shelled
   and deveined

2 tbsp snipped fresh chives

2 tsp light soy sauce

dash of chili sauce

2 tbsp vegetable oil

VARIATION

You could add extra flavor
to the omelet by stirring in
3 tbsp of finely chopped fresh
cilantro or 1 tsp
of sesame seeds with the
fresh chives in step 2.

1 Lightly beat the eggs in a large
bowl. Add the shredded chicken
and jumbo shrimps, and mix well.

2 Stir in the snipped chives, light
soy sauce, and chili sauce, mixing
well to blend all the ingredients.

3 Heat the oil in a large, heavy-
bottomed skillet over a medium
heat. Pour in the egg mixture, tilting
the pan to coat the bottom evenly
and completely.

4 Cook over a medium heat, gently
stirring the omelet with a fork,
until the surface is just set and the
underside is golden brown.

5 When the omelet is set, slide it
out of the pan with the aid of a
spatula, then cut into squares or slices
and serve immediately.

sesame ginger chicken

serves four

1 lb 2 oz/500 g boneless
  chicken breasts

dipping sauce, to serve

MARINADE

1 garlic clove, minced

1 shallot, chopped very finely

2 tbsp sesame oil

1 tbsp fish sauce or light soy sauce

finely grated peel of 1 lime or
  ½ lemon

2 tbsp lime juice or lemon juice

1 tsp sesame seeds

2 tsp finely grated fresh gingerroot

2 tsp chopped fresh mint

salt and pepper

1 To make the marinade, put the garlic, shallot, sesame oil, fish sauce or soy sauce, lime or lemon peel and juice, sesame seeds, ginger, and chopped mint into a large non-metallic bowl. Season with a little salt and pepper and stir well until all the ingredients are mixed thoroughly.

2 Using a sharp knife, remove the skin from the chicken breasts and discard. Cut the flesh into chunks.

3 Add the chicken to the marinade, stirring to coat the chicken completely in the mixture. Cover with plastic wrap and chill in the refrigerator for at least 2 hours, so all the flavors are absorbed.

4 Thread the chicken onto presoaked wooden satay sticks. Put them on the rack of a broiler pan and baste with the marinade.

5 Cook the kabobs under a preheated medium-hot broiler for about 8–10 minutes. Turn the kabobs frequently, basting with the remaining marinade.

6 Put the chicken kabobs onto a large serving plate and serve immediately with a dipping sauce.

chicken or beef satay

serves six

4 skinned, boneless chicken breasts
　　or 1 lb 10 oz/750 g rump
　　steak, trimmed

MARINADE

1 small onion, chopped finely

1 garlic clove, minced

1-inch/2.5-cm piece fresh
　　gingerroot, grated

2 tbsp dark soy sauce

2 tsp chili powder

1 tsp ground coriander

2 tsp dark brown sugar

1 tbsp lemon or lime juice

1 tbsp vegetable oil

SAUCE

1¼ cups coconut milk

⅓ cup crunchy peanut butter

1 tbsp fish sauce

1 tsp lemon or lime juice

salt and pepper

1 Using a sharp knife, trim any fat from the chicken or beef and discard. Cut the meat into thin strips, about 3-inches/7-cm long.

2 To make the marinade, put all the ingredients in a shallow dish and mix well. Add the chicken or beef strips and turn in the marinade until well coated. Cover with plastic wrap and let marinate in the refrigerator for 2 hours, or preferably overnight .

3 Remove the meat from the marinade and thread the pieces, concertina style, onto presoaked bamboo or thin wooden skewers.

4 Put the chicken and beef satays under a preheated medium-hot broiler and cook for 8–10 minutes, turning and brushing occasionally with the marinade, until cooked through.

5 To make the sauce. Mix the coconut milk, peanut butter, fish sauce and lemon or lime juice in a pan. Bring to a boil and cook for 3 minutes. Season to taste with salt and pepper.

6 Pour the sauce into a serving bowl and serve with the satays.

Fish & Seafood

The wealth of species and flavors of fish and seafood that the world's oceans and rivers provide is immense. Each country combines its local catch with the region's favorite herb and spices to create a variety of dishes. All of the recipes featured here are easy to prepare and delicious to eat. Moreover, not only are fish and seafood quick to cook, but they are packed full of nutritional goodness. Naturally low in fat, yet rich in minerals and proteins, fish and seafood are important to help balance any diet. The variety of fish and fish prices helps us to choose dishes to suit both mood and pocket.

smoked trout & apple salad

serves four

2 orange-red eating apples

2 tbsp French dressing

1½ cups arugula

1 smoked trout, about 6 oz/175 g

Melba Toast, to serve

   (see Cook's Tip)

HORSERADISH DRESSING

½ cup lowfat plain yogurt

½–1 tsp lemon juice

1 tbsp horseradish sauce

milk, optional

salt and pepper

TO GARNISH

1 tbsp chopped fresh chives

fresh chive flowers, optional

COOK'S TIP

To make Melba Toast, toast medium sliced bread, then cut off the crusts, and carefully slice in half horizontally with a sharp knife. Cut in half diagonally and put toasted side down in a warmed oven for about 15–20 minutes until the edges start to curl and the toast is crisp.

1 Leaving the skin on, cut the apples into fourths and remove the cores. Slice the apples into a bowl and toss in the French dressing to prevent them turning brown.

2 Arrange the arugula on 4 large serving plates.

3 Skin the trout and take out the bone. Carefully remove any fine bones that remain, using your fingers or tweezers. Flake the trout into fairly large pieces and arrange with the apple between the arugula.

4 To make the horseradish dressing, whisk all the ingredients together, adding a little milk if too thick, then drizzle over the trout. Sprinkle the snipped chives and flowers (if using) over the trout and serve with Melba Toast (see Cook's Tip).

sweet & sour tuna salad

serves four

2 tbsp olive oil

1 onion, chopped

2 garlic cloves, chopped

2 zucchini, sliced

4 tomatoes, peeled

14 oz/400 g canned small cannellini
   beans, drained and rinsed

10 pitted ripe black olives, halved

1 tbsp capers

1 tsp superfine sugar

1 tbsp whole-grain mustard

1 tbsp white wine vinegar

7 oz/200 g canned tuna, drained

2 tbsp chopped fresh parsley, plus
   extra to garnish

crusty bread, to serve

1 Heat the oil in a large, heavy-bottomed skillet over a low heat. Add the onion and garlic and cook, stirring occasionally, for 5 minutes, or until softened, but not browned.

2 Add the zucchini slices and cook, stirring occasionally, for an additional 3 minutes.

3 Cut the tomatoes in half, then into thin wedges.

4 Add the tomatoes to the skillet with the beans, olives, capers, sugar, mustard, and vinegar.

5 Simmer for 2 minutes, stirring gently, then let cool slightly.

6 Flake the tuna and stir it into the bean mixture with the parsley. Transfer to 4 serving plates, garnish with the extra chopped parsley, and serve warm with crusty bread.

tuna, bean & anchovy salad

serves four

1 lb 2 oz/500 g tomatoes

7 oz/200 g canned tuna, drained

2 tbsp chopped fresh parsley

½ cucumber

1 small red onion

8 oz/225 g cooked green beans

1 small red bell pepper, seeded

1 small crisp lettuce

6 tbsp Italian-style dressing

3 hard-cooked eggs

2 oz/55 g canned anchovy
   fillets, drained

12 pitted ripe black olives

1 Cut the tomatoes into wedges, flake the tuna and put both into a large bowl with the chopped parsley.

2 Cut the cucumber into slices. Slice the onion. Add the cucumber and onion to the bowl.

3 Cut the green beans in half, chop the bell pepper, and add both to the bowl with the lettuce leaves. Pour over the dressing and toss to mix, then spoon into a salad bowl. Shell the eggs and cut into fourths and add to the salad with the anchovies. Sprinkle over the olives and serve.

mussel salad

1 Put the bell peppers, skin-side up, on a broiler rack and cook under a preheated broiler for 8–10 minutes, or until the skin is charred and blistered and the flesh is soft. Remove from the broiler with tongs, put into a bowl, and cover with plastic wrap. Set aside for 10 minutes, or until cool enough to handle, then peel off the skins.

2 Slice the bell pepper flesh into thin strips and put into a bowl. Gently stir in the shelled mussels.

3 To make the dressing, whisk the oil, lemon juice and peel, honey, mustard, and chives together until well blended. Season to taste with salt and pepper. Add the bell pepper and mussel mixture and toss until coated.

4 Remove the central core of the radicchio and shred the leaves. Put into a serving bowl with the arugula and toss together.

5 Pile the mussel mixture into the center of the leaves and arrange the green-lipped mussels in their shells around the edge. Garnish with lemon peel and serve with crusty bread.

neapolitan seafood salad

serves four

1 lb/450 g prepared squid, cut
   into strips

1 lb 10 oz/750 g cooked mussels

1 lb/450 g cooked cockles in brine

⅝ cup white wine

1¼ cups olive oil

2 cups dried campanelle or other
   small pasta shapes

juice of 1 lemon

1 bunch fresh chives, snipped

1 bunch fresh parsley,
   chopped finely

4 large tomatoes

mixed salad greens

salt and pepper

1 fresh basil sprig, to garnish

1 Put the seafood into a large bowl, pour over the wine and half the oil, then set aside for 6 hours.

2 Put the seafood mixture into a pan and simmer over a low heat for 10 minutes. Let cool.

3 Bring a large pan of lightly salted water to a boil over a medium heat. Add the pasta and 1 tablespoon of the remaining oil and cook until done. Drain and refresh in cold water.

4 Strain off about half the cooking liquid from the seafood and discard the rest. Mix in the lemon juice, chives, parsley, and the remaining oil. Season with salt and pepper. Drain the pasta and add to the seafood.

5 Cut the tomatoes into fourths. Shred the salad greens and arrange them at the bottom of a salad bowl. Spoon in the salad and garnish with the tomatoes and a basil sprig.

seafood stir-fry

serves four

3½ oz/100 g small, thin asparagus
  spears, trimmed

1 tbsp corn oil

2.5-cm/1-inch piece fresh
  gingerroot, cut into thin strips

1 medium leek, shredded

2 medium carrots, julienned

3½ oz/100 g baby corn, cut into
  fourths lengthwise

2 tbsp light soy sauce

1 tbsp oyster sauce

1 tsp honey

1 lb/450 g cooked, assorted
  shellfish, thawed if frozen

freshly cooked egg noodles,
  to serve

TO GARNISH

4 large cooked shrimp

1 small bunch fresh chives, snipped

1 Bring a small pan of water to a boil over a medium heat. Add the asparagus and blanch for 1–2 minutes. Drain, set aside and keep warm.

2 Heat a large wok over a medium heat. Add the oil and when hot, add the ginger, leek, carrot, and corn. Cook for about 3 minutes.

3 Add the soy sauce, oyster sauce, and honey to the wok. Stir in the shellfish and cook for 2–3 minutes, or until the vegetables are just tender and the shellfish are thoroughly heated through. Add the blanched asparagus and cook for an additional 2 minutes.

4 To serve, pile the cooked noodles onto 4 warmed serving plates and spoon over the seafood and vegetables. Garnish with a large shrimp and the chives, then serve.

poached salmon with penne

serves four

4 x 10 oz/275 g fresh salmon steaks

4 tbsp butter

¾ cup dry white wine

pinch of sea salt

8 peppercorns

1 fresh dill sprig

1 fresh tarragon sprig

1 lemon, sliced

4 cups dried penne

1 tbsp olive oil

2 tbsp butter

¼ cup all-purpose flour

⅔ cup warm milk

juice and finely grated peel of
2 lemons

1¼ cups arugula, chopped

salt and pepper

slices of lemon, to garnish

1 Put the salmon into a large, non-stick skillet. Add the butter, wine, sea salt, peppercorns, dill, tarragon, and lemon. Cover, bring to a boil over a low heat, and cook for 10 minutes.

2 Using a spatula, carefully remove the salmon. Strain and set aside the cooking liquid. Remove the salmon skin and center bones and discard. Put the salmon into a warmed dish, cover and keep warm.

3 Meanwhile, bring a pan of lightly salted water to a boil over a medium heat. Add the pasta and 1 teaspoon of the oil and cook for about 12 minutes, or until done. Drain and sprinkle over the remaining oil. Put into a warmed serving dish, top with the salmon and keep warm.

4 To make the sauce, melt the butter over a low heat. Stir in the flour for 2 minutes, then stir in the milk and 7 tablespoons of the cooking liquid. Add the lemon juice and peel and cook, stirring, for 10 minutes.

5 Add the arugula to the sauce, stir gently and season to taste with salt and pepper.

6 Pour the sauce over the salmon, garnish with slices of lemon and serve immediately.

trout with smoked bacon

serves four

1 tbsp butter for greasing

4 x 9½ oz/275 g trout, gutted
   and cleaned

12 canned anchovy fillets in oil,
   drained and chopped

2 apples, peeled, cored, and sliced

4 fresh mint sprigs

juice of 1 lemon

12 slices rindless, smoked fatty bacon

1 lb/450 g dried tagliatelle

1 tsp olive oil

salt and pepper

TO GARNISH

2 apples, cored and sliced

4 fresh mint sprigs

1 Grease a large cookie sheet with the butter.

2 Open up the cavities of each trout and rinse with warm salt water.

3 Season each cavity with salt and pepper. Divide the anchovies, sliced apples, and mint sprigs between each of the cavities, then sprinkle the lemon juice into each cavity.

4 Carefully cover the whole of each trout, except the head and tail, with 3 slices of smoked bacon in a spiral shape.

5 Arrange the trout on the cookie sheet with the loose ends of bacon tucked underneath. Season with pepper to taste and cook in a preheated oven at 400°F/ 200°C, for 20 minutes, turning the trout over after 10 minutes.

6 Meanwhile, bring a large pan of lightly salted water to a boil over a medium heat. Add the pasta and oil and cook for about 12 minutes, or until done. Drain the pasta and keep warm.

7 Remove the trout from the oven. Transfer the pasta to 4 warmed serving plates and arrange the trout on top. Garnish with sliced apples and mint sprigs, and serve immediately.

3

4

fillets of red snapper & pasta

serves four

2 lb 4 oz/1 kg red snapper fillets

1¼ cups dry white wine

4 shallots, chopped finely

1 garlic clove, minced

3 tbsp finely chopped mixed
   fresh herbs

finely grated peel and juice of
   1 lemon

pinch of freshly grated nutmeg

3 canned anchovy fillets,
   chopped coarsely

2 tbsp heavy cream

1 tsp cornstarch

1 lb/450 g dried vermicelli

1 tsp olive oil

salt and pepper

TO GARNISH

1 fresh mint sprig

slices of lemon

strips of lemon peel

1 Put the red snapper fillets into a large casserole dish. Pour over the wine and add the shallots, garlic, herbs, lemon peel and juice, nutmeg, and anchovies. Season to taste with salt and pepper. Cover and cook in a preheated oven at 350°F/180°C, for about 35 minutes.

2 Transfer the snapper to a warmed dish. Set aside and keep warm.

3 Pour the cooking liquid into a pan and bring to a boil over a low heat. Simmer gently for 25 minutes, until reduced by half. Mix the cream and cornstarch together and stir into the sauce to thicken.

4 Bring a pan of lightly salted water to a boil over a medium heat. Add the pasta and oil and cook for 8–10 minutes, or until done. Drain the pasta thoroughly and transfer to a warmed serving dish.

5 Arrange the red snapper fillets on top of the pasta and pour the sauce over them. Garnish with a mint sprig, slices of lemon, and strips of lemon peel. Serve immediately.

101

rice with crab & mussels

serves four

1½ cups long-grain rice

6 oz/175 g white crab meat, fresh,
    canned or frozen (thawed if
    frozen), or 8 crab sticks, thawed
    if frozen

2 tbsp sesame or corn oil

1-inch/2.5-cm piece fresh
    gingerroot, grated

4 scallions, thinly sliced diagonally

4½ oz/125 g snow peas, cut into
    2–3 pieces

½ tsp turmeric

1 tsp ground cumin

14 oz/400 g canned mussels, well
    drained, or 12 oz/350 g frozen
    mussels, thawed

15 oz/350 g canned bean sprouts,
    well drained

salt and pepper

1 Bring a large pan of lightly salted water to a boil over a medium heat. Add the rice and cook for about 15 minutes. Drain and keep warm.

2 Extract the crab meat, if using fresh crab. Flake the crab meat or cut the crab sticks into 3–4 pieces.

3 Heat a large wok over a high heat. Add the oil and when hot, add the ginger and scallions and cook for 1–2 minutes. Add the snow peas and continue to cook for an additional 1 minute. Sprinkle over the turmeric, cumin, then season to taste with salt and pepper. Mix thoroughly.

4 Add the crab meat and mussels to the wok and cook, stirring, for 1 minute. Stir in the cooked rice and bean sprouts, and cook for 2 minutes, or until hot and well mixed.

5 Adjust the seasoning to taste, if necessary. Transfer to a large serving dish and serve immediately.

flounder fillets with grapes

serves four

1 lb 2 oz/500 g flounder fillets, skinned

4 scallions, white and green parts,
 sliced diagonally

½ cup dry white wine

1 tbsp cornstarch

2 tbsp skim milk

2 tbsp chopped fresh dill

4 tbsp heavy cream

4½ oz/125 g seedless green grapes

1 tsp lemon juice

salt and pepper

fresh dill sprigs, to garnish

TO SERVE

freshly cooked basmati rice

zucchini ribbons

COOK'S TIP

Dill has a fairly strong anise
flavor that goes well with fish.
The feathery leaves are attractive
when used as a garnish.

---

1 Using a sharp knife, cut the
fish fillets into strips, about
1½-inches/4-cm long and put into a
skillet with the scallions and wine.
season to taste with salt and pepper.

2 Bring to a boil over a medium
heat, cover, and simmer for about
4 minutes. Carefully transfer the fish to
a warmed serving dish. Cover and
keep warm while you make the sauce.

3 Mix the cornstarch and milk
together, then add to the skillet
with the dill and cream. Bring to a boil
over a high heat, and boil, stirring, for
2 minutes until thickened.

4 Add the grapes and lemon juice
and heat through gently for
1—2 minutes, then pour over the fish.
Garnish with dill sprigs and serve with
cooked rice and zucchini ribbons.

pasta & anchovy sauce

serves four

6 tbsp olive oil

2 garlic cloves, minced

2 oz/55 g canned anchovy
  fillets, drained

1 lb/450 g dried spaghetti

¼ cup Pesto Sauce (see page 227)

2 tbsp finely chopped fresh oregano

1 cup freshly grated Parmesan
  cheese, plus extra for serving

salt and pepper

2 fresh oregano sprigs, to garnish

1 Set aside 1 tablespoon of the oil
and heat the remainder in a small
pan over a medium heat. Add the
garlic and cook for 3 minutes.

2 Reduce the heat, stir in the
anchovies and cook, stirring
occasionally, until the anchovies
have disintegrated.

3 Bring a pan of lightly salted water
to a boil over a medium heat.
Add the pasta and remaining oil and
cook for 8–10 minutes, or until done.

4 Add the Pesto Sauce (see page
227) and chopped fresh oregano
to the anchovy mixture, then season
with pepper to taste.

5 Using a slotted spoon, drain the
pasta and transfer to a warmed
serving dish. Pour the Pesto Sauce over
the pasta, then sprinkle over the grated
Parmesan cheese.

6 Garnish with oregano sprigs and
serve immediately with extra
Parmesan cheese.

seafood medley

serves four

12 raw jumbo shrimp

12 raw shrimp

1 lb/450 g fillet of sea bream

4 tbsp butter

12 scallops, shelled

4½ oz/125 g freshwater shrimp

juice and finely grated peel of

   1 lemon

pinch of saffron powder or threads

4 cups vegetable bouillon

⅔ cup rose petal vinegar

   (see Cook' Tip)

4 cups dried farfalle

1 tsp olive oil

⅔ cup white wine

1 tbsp pink peppercorns

4 oz/115 g baby carrots

⅔ cup heavy cream

salt and pepper

COOK'S TIP

To make rose petal vinegar,
infuse the petals of 8 pesticide-
free roses in ⅔ cup white wine
vinegar for 48 hours. Prepare
well in advance to
reduce the preparation time.

1 Shell and devein the jumbo
shrimp and shrimp. Using a sharp
knife, thinly slice the sea bream. Melt
the butter in a large skillet over a
medium heat. Add the sea bream,
scallops, jumbo shrimp, and shrimp
and cook for 1–2 minutes.

2 Season with pepper to taste. Add
the lemon juice and grated peel.
Very carefully add a pinch of saffron
powder or a few strands of saffron to
the cooking juices (not to the seafood).

3 Remove the seafood from the
pan, set aside, and keep warm.

4 Return the pan to the heat and
add the bouillon. Bring to a boil
over a medium heat and reduce by one
third. Add the vinegar and cook for
4 minutes, or until reduced.

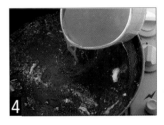

5 Bring a pan of lightly salted water
to a boil over a medium heat.
Add the pasta and oil and cook for
8–10 minutes, or until done. Drain the
pasta thoroughly, transfer to a serving
plate and top with the seafood.

6 Add the wine, peppercorns, and
carrots to the pan and reduce the
sauce for 6 minutes. Add the cream
and simmer for 2 minutes.

7 Pour the sauce over the seafood
and pasta and serve immediately.

spaghetti & seafood sauce

serves four

8 oz/225 g dried spaghetti, broken
into 6-inch/15-cm lengths

1 tbsp olive oil

1¼ cups chicken bouillon

1 tsp lemon juice

1 small cauliflower, cut
into flowerets

2 carrots, sliced thinly

4 oz/115 g snow peas

4 tbsp butter

1 onion, sliced

8 oz/225 g zucchini, sliced

1 garlic clove, chopped

12 oz/350 g frozen, cooked, shelled
shrimp, thawed

2 tbsp chopped fresh parsley

¼ cup freshly grated
Parmesan cheese

½ tsp paprika

salt and pepper

1 Bring a pan of lightly salted water to a boil over a medium heat. Add the pasta and cook until done. Drain the pasta thoroughly and return to the pan. Toss with the oil, cover, and keep warm.

2 Bring the chicken bouillon and lemon juice to a boil. Add the cauliflower and carrot and cook for 3–4 minutes. Remove from the pan and set aside. Add the snow peas to the pan and cook for 1–2 minutes. Set aside with the other vegetables.

3 Melt half the butter in a skillet over a medium heat. Add the onion and zucchini and cook for about 3 minutes. Add the garlic and shrimp and cook until heated through.

4 Stir in the reserved vegetables and heat through. Season to taste with salt and pepper and stir in the remaining butter.

5 Transfer the pasta to a warmed serving dish. Pour over the sauce and add the chopped parsley. Toss well with 2 forks until the pasta is coated. Sprinkle over the Parmesan cheese and paprika, then serve immediately.

mussel & scallop spaghetti

serves four

8 oz/225 g dried
   whole-wheat spaghetti

2 slices rindless, lean back
   bacon, chopped

2 shallots, chopped finely

2 celery stalk, chopped finely

⅔ cup dry white wine

⅔ cup fish bouillon

1 lb 2 oz/500 g fresh
   mussels, prepared

8 oz/225 g shelled queen or China
   bay scallops

1 tbsp chopped fresh parsley

salt and pepper

1 Bring a large pan of lightly salted water to a boil over a medium heat. Add the pasta and cook for about 10 minutes, or until done.

2 Meanwhile, dry-fry the bacon in a large non-stick skillet for about 2–3 minutes. Stir in the shallots, celery, and wine. Simmer gently for 5 minutes, or until softened.

3 Add the bouillon, mussels, and scallops, cover and cook for an additional 6–7 minutes. Discard any mussels that remain unopened.

4 Drain the pasta and add to the skillet. Add the parsley, season to taste with salt and pepper, and toss together. Cook for 1–2 minutes. Pile onto warmed serving plates, spooning over the juices. Serve.

noodles with shrimp

serves four

8 oz/225 g thin egg noodles

2 tbsp groundnut oil

1 garlic clove, minced

½ tsp ground star anise

1 bunch scallions, cut into
2-inch/5-cm pieces

24 raw jumbo shrimp, shelled, with
tails intact

2 tbsp light soy sauce

2 tsp lime juice

slices of lime, to garnish

COOK'S TIP

If fresh egg noodles are
available, these require very little
cooking. Simply put into boiling
water for about 3 minutes, then
drain and toss in oil. Noodles can
be boiled and eaten plain, or
cooked with meat and
vegetables for a light meal.

1 Bring a pan of water to a boil over a medium heat. Add the noodles and blanch for 2–3 minutes.

2 Drain the noodles thoroughly, rinse under cold running water and drain again. Keep warm and set aside until required.

3 Heat a large wok over a high heat. Add the groundnut oil and when almost smoking, add the garlic and ground star anise, and cook for 30 seconds.

4 Add the scallions and jumbo shrimp to the wok, and cook for 2–3 minutes.

5 Stir in the light soy sauce, lime juice, and noodles, and mix well.

6 Cook the mixture in the wok for about 1 minute until thoroughly heated through and all the ingredients are incorporated.

7 Spoon the noodle and shrimp mixture into 4 warmed serving dishes and garnish with slices lime. Serve immediately.

cellophane noodles & shrimp

serves four

6 oz/175 g cellophane noodles

1 tbsp vegetable oil

1 garlic clove, minced

2 tsp grated fresh gingerroot

24 raw jumbo shrimp, shelled
and deveined

1 red bell pepper, seeded and
sliced thinly

1 green bell pepper, seeded and
sliced thinly

1 onion, chopped

2 tbsp light soy sauce

juice of 1 orange

2 tsp wine vinegar

pinch of brown sugar

⅔ cup fish bouillon

1 tbsp cornstarch

2 tsp water

slices of orange, to garnish

1 Bring a pan of water to a boil over a medium heat. Add the noodles and blanch for 1 minute. Drain well, rinse, and drain again.

2 Heat a large wok and over a high heat. Add the oil and when hot, add the garlic and ginger, and cook for 30 seconds.

3 Add the shrimp and cook for 2 minutes. Remove with a slotted spoon and keep warm.

4 Add the bell peppers and onion, and cook for 2 minutes. Stir in the soy sauce, orange juice, vinegar, sugar, and bouillon. Return the shrimp to the wok and cook for 8–10 minutes.

5 Blend the cornstarch with the water and stir into the wok. Bring to a boil over a medium heat. Add the noodles and cook for 1–2 minutes. Transfer to 4 warmed bowls, garnish with orange slices and serve.

sweet & sour noodles

serves four

3 tbsp fish sauce

2 tbsp distilled white vinegar

2 tbsp palm or superfine sugar

2 tbsp tomato paste

2 tbsp corn oil

3 cloves garlic, minced

12 oz/350 g rice noodles, soaked in
boiling water for 5 minutes

8 scallions, sliced

2 carrots, grated

1½ cups bean sprouts

2 eggs, beaten

8 oz/225 g shelled king shrimp

½ cup chopped peanuts

1 tsp chili flakes, to garnish

4 Add the scallions, carrots, and bean sprouts to the wok and cook for 2–3 minutes.

5 Move the stir-fry mixture to one side of the wok, add the beaten eggs to the empty part of the wok and cook until the egg sets. Add the noodles, shrimp, and peanuts to the wok and mix well. Transfer to 4 large, warmed serving dishes and garnish with chili flakes. Serve immediately.

COOK'S TIP
Chili flakes may be found
in the spice section of large
food stores.

1 Mix the fish sauce, vinegar, sugar, and tomato paste together.

2 Heat a large wok over a high heat. Add the oil and when hot, add the garlic. Cook for 30 seconds.

3 Drain the noodles thoroughly and add them to the wok together with the fish sauce and tomato paste mixture. Mix well.

seafood chow mein

serves four

3 oz/85 g squid, cleaned

3–4 fresh scallops

3 oz/85 g raw shrimp, shelled

½ egg white, beaten lightly

1 tbsp cornstarch paste
  (see page 7)

9½ oz/275 g egg noodles

5–6 tbsp vegetable oil

2 tbsp light soy sauce

2 oz/55 g snow peas

½ tsp salt

½ tsp sugar

1 tsp Chinese rice wine

2 scallions, shredded finely

few drops of sesame oil

1 Open up the squid and score the inside in a criss-cross pattern, then cut into pieces about the size of a postage stamp. Soak the squid in a bowl of boiling water until all the pieces curl up. Rinse in cold water and drain.

2 Cut each scallop into 3–4 slices. Cut the shrimp in half lengthwise, if large. Mix the scallops and shrimp together with the egg white, and cornstarch paste.

3 Bring a large pan of water to a boil over a medium heat. Add the noodles and cook according to the package instructions. Drain and rinse under cold water, then drain again. Toss with about 1 tablespoon of oil.

4 Heat a wok over a high heat. Add 3 tablespoons of oil and when hot, add the noodles and 1 tablespoon of soy sauce. Cook for 2–3 minutes. Transfer to a large serving dish.

5 Heat the remaining oil in the wok and add the snow peas and seafood. Cook for 2 minutes, then add the salt, sugar, Chinese rice wine, remaining soy sauce, and about half the scallions. Blend and add a little water, if necessary. Pour the seafood mixture on top of the noodles and sprinkle with sesame oil. Garnish with the remaining scallions and serve.

chile shrimp noodles

serves four

2 tbsp light soy sauce
1 tbsp lime or lemon juice
1 tbsp fish sauce
4½ oz/125 g firm beancurd, cut into
   chunks (drained weight)
4½ oz/125 g cellophane noodles
2 tbsp sesame oil
4 shallots, sliced finely
2 garlic cloves, minced
1 small fresh red chili, seeded and
   chopped finely
2 celery stalks, sliced finely
2 carrots, sliced finely
⅔ cup cooked small shrimp, shelled
1 cup bean sprouts
TO GARNISH
celery leaves
fresh chiles

1 Mix the light soy sauce, lime or lemon juice, and fish sauce together in a small bowl. Add the beancurd cubes and toss until coated in the mixture. Cover and set aside for 15 minutes.

2 Put the noodles into a large bowl and pour over enough warm water to cover. Let soak for 5 minutes, then drain thoroughly.

3 Heat a large wok over a high heat. Add the sesame oil and when hot, add the shallots, garlic, and red chile, and stir-fry for 1 minute.

4 Add the sliced celery and carrots to the wok and cook, stirring, for an additional 2–3 minutes.

5 Tip the drained noodles into the wok and cook, stirring, for about 2 minutes, then add the shrimp, bean sprouts, and beancurd with the soy sauce mixture. Cook over a medium high heat for 2–3 minutes, or until heated through.

6 Transfer the mixture to 4 serving bowls, garnish with celery leaves and chiles and serve.

thai-style shrimp noodles

serves four

9 oz/250 g thin glass noodles

2 tbsp corn oil

1 onion, sliced

2 fresh red chiles, seeded and
chopped very finely

4 lime leaves, shredded thinly

1 tbsp fresh cilantro

2 tbsp palm or superfine sugar

2 tbsp fish sauce

1 lb/450 g raw jumbo
shrimp, shelled

1 Put the noodles into a large bowl, pour over enough boiling water to cover and let stand for 5 minutes. Drain thoroughly and set aside.

2 Heat a large wok over a high heat, then add the oil.

3 When the oil is very hot, add the onion, red chiles, and lime leaves and cook for 1 minute.

4 Add the cilantro, palm or superfine sugar, fish sauce, and shrimp to the wok and cook for an additional 2 minutes, or until the shrimp turn pink.

5 Add the drained noodles to the wok, toss to mix thoroughly, and cook for 1–2 minutes, or until heated through.

6 Transfer the noodles and shrimp to 4 large, warmed serving bowls and serve immediately.

COOK'S TIP

If you cannot buy raw jumbo shrimp, substitute with some cooked shrimp, thawed if frozen, and cook them with the cooked noodles in step 5 for 1 minute only, just to heat them through.

fried rice & shrimp

serves four

1½ cups long-grain rice

2 eggs

4 tsp cold water

salt and pepper

3 tbsp corn oil

4 scallions, thinly sliced diagonally

1 garlic clove, minced

4½ oz/125 g closed cup or white
  mushrooms, sliced thinly

2 tbsp oyster or anchovy sauce

7 oz/200 g canned water chestnuts,
  drained and sliced

9 oz/250 g shelled shrimp, thawed
  if frozen

1 cup arugula, chopped coarsely

1 Bring a large pan of lightly salted water to a boil over a medium heat. Add the rice and cook for about 15 minutes. Drain and keep warm.

2 Beat each egg separately with 2 teaspoons of cold water and season to taste with salt and pepper.

3 Heat a large wok over a high heat. Add 2 teaspoons of the oil and carefully swirl it around until hot. Pour in the first egg, swirl it around and let cook, undisturbed, until set. Transfer to a plate or board and repeat with the second egg. Cut the omelets into 1-inch/2.5-cm squares.

4 Heat the remaining oil in the wok and when really hot, add the scallions and garlic. Cook for 1 minute. Add the mushrooms and continue to cook for an additional 2 minutes.

5 Stir in the oyster or anchovy sauce and season, if necessary. Add the water chestnuts and shrimp, and cook for 2 minutes.

6 Stir in the cooked rice and cooked for 1 minute, then add the arugula and omelet squares and cook for an additional 1-2 minutes, or until piping hot. Serve immediately.

aromatic seafood rice

serves four

1¼ cups basmati rice

2 tbsp ghee or vegetable oil

1 onion, chopped

1 garlic clove, minced

1 tsp cumin seeds

½–1 tsp chilli powder

4 cloves

1 cinnamon stick or a piece of
    cassia bark

2 tsp curry paste

8 oz/225 g shelled shrimp

1 lb 2 oz/500 g white fish fillets
    (such as angler fish, cod, or
    haddock), skinned and boned,
    and cut into bite-size pieces

2½ cups boiling water

⅓ cup frozen peas

⅓ cup frozen corn

1–2 tbsp lime juice

2 tbsp toasted shredded coconut

salt and pepper

TO GARNISH

fresh cilantro sprigs

2 slices of lime

1 Put the rice in a strainer and wash well in cold water until the water runs clear, then drain thoroughly.

2 Heat the ghee or oil in a pan over a low heat. Add the onion, garlic, spices, and curry paste, and cook gently for 1 minute.

3 Stir in the rice and mix well until coated in the spiced oil. Add the shrimp and white fish. Season well with salt and pepper. Stir lightly, then pour in the boiling water.

4 Cover and cook for 10 minutes. Add the peas and corn, cover and continue cooking for an additional 8 minutes. Remove from the heat and let stand for 10 minutes.

5 Uncover the pan, fluff up the rice with a fork and transfer to a warmed serving platter.

6 Sprinkle the dish with the lime juice and toasted coconut, and garnish with cilantro sprigs and the lime slices. Serve immediately.

oyster sauce noodles

serves four

9 oz/250 g egg noodles

1 lb/450 g chicken thighs

2 tbsp groundnut oil

3½ oz/100 g carrots, sliced

3 tbsp oyster sauce

2 eggs

3 tbsp cold water

1 Put the egg noodles into a large bowl or dish. Pour over enough boiling water to cover and let stand for 10 minutes.

2 Meanwhile, remove the skin from the chicken thighs and discard. Cut the chicken flesh into small pieces with a sharp knife.

3 Heat a large wok over a high heat, then add the oil.

4 When the oil is hot, add the chicken and carrot slices, and cook for about 5 minutes.

5 Drain the noodles thoroughly, then add to the wok. Cook for an additional 2–3 minutes, or until the noodles are heated through.

6 Beat the oyster sauce, eggs and 3 tablespoons of cold water together. Drizzle the mixture over the noodles and cook for an additional 2–3 minutes, or until the eggs set. Transfer to 4 warmed serving bowls and serve immediately.

VARIATION

Flavor the eggs with soy sauce or hoisin sauce as an alternative to the oyster sauce, if you prefer.

shrimp pasta bake

serves four

2 cups dried tricolor pasta shapes

1 tbsp vegetable oil

2½ cups sliced white mushrooms

1 bunch scallions, trimmed
and chopped

14 oz/400 g canned tuna in brine,
drained and flaked

6 oz/175 g shelled shrimp, thawed
if frozen

2 tbsp cornstarch

1¾ cups skim milk

4 tomatoes, sliced thinly

½ cup fresh bread crumbs

¼ cup freshly grated reduced-fat
cheddar cheese

salt and pepper

1 Bring a large pan of lightly salted water to a boil over a medium heat. Add the pasta and cook for 8–10 minutes, or until done. Drain the pasta thoroughly.

2 Meanwhile, heat the oil in a large skillet over a low heat. Add the mushrooms and all but a handful of the scallions and cook, stirring frequently, for about 4–5 minutes, or until softened.

3 Put the cooked pasta into a bowl and mix in the mushroom and scallion mixture, tuna, and shrimp.

4 Blend the cornstarch with a little milk to make a smooth paste. Pour the remaining milk into a pan and stir in the paste. Heat, stirring constantly, until the sauce starts to thicken. Season well with salt and pepper. Add the sauce to the pasta mixture and mix thoroughly. Transfer to an ovenproof gratin dish and put on a cookie sheet.

5 Arrange the tomato slices over the pasta and sprinkle with the bread crumbs and cheese. Cook in a preheated oven at 375°F/190°C, for 25–30 minutes, or until golden brown. Garnished with the scallions and serve.

indian cod with tomatoes

serves four

3 tbsp vegetable oil

4 cod steaks, 1-inch/2.5-cm thick

1 onion, chopped finely

2 garlic cloves, minced

1 red bell pepper, seeded
   and chopped

1 tsp ground coriander

1 tsp ground cumin

1 tsp turmeric

½ tsp garam masala

14 oz/400 g canned
   chopped tomatoes

⅔ cup coconut milk

1–2 tbsp chopped fresh cilantro
   or parsley

salt and pepper

1 Heat the oil in a skillet over a
medium heat. Add the fish steaks,
season with salt and pepper and cook
until brown, but not cooked through.
Remove from the skillet and set aside.

2 Add the onion, garlic, red bell
pepper, and spices and cook
gently for 2 minutes, stirring frequently.
Add the tomatoes, bring to a boil over
a low heat and simmer for 5 minutes.

3 Add the fish steaks to the skillet
and simmer gently for 8 minutes,
or until the fish is cooked through.

4 Remove from the skillet and keep
warm in a serving dish. Add the
coconut milk and cilantro or parsley to
the skillet and heat gently.

5 Spoon the sauce over the fish
steaks and serve immediately.

smoky fish kabobs

serves four

12 oz/350 g smoked cod fillet

12 oz/350 g cod fillet

8 large raw shrimp

8 bay leaves

fresh dill sprigs, to garnish (optional)

MARINADE

4 tbsp corn oil, plus a little
    for brushing

2 tbsp lemon or lime juice

grated peel of ½ lemon or lime

¼ tsp dried dill

salt and pepper

1 Skin both types of cod and cut the flesh into bite-size pieces. Shell the shrimp, leaving just the tail.

2 To make the marinade, mix the oil, lemon juice and peel, and dill, together in a shallow dish. Season to taste with salt and pepper.

3 Put the prepared fish in the marinade and stir until the fish is coated on all sides. Let marinate in the refrigerator for 1–4 hours.

4 Thread the fish onto 4 metal skewers, alternating the fish with the shrimp and bay leaves.

5 Cover a barbecue grill rack with oiled foil and put the skewers on top. Cook the skewers over medium-hot coals for 5-10 minutes, basting with the marinade. Turn once. Garnish the skewers with fresh dill and serve.

125

scallop kabobs

1 Soak 8 wooden skewers in warm water for at least 10 minutes before you use them to prevent burning on the barbecue.

2 Mix the lime juice and peel, lemon grass, garlic and chile together in a pestle and mortar or spice grinder to make a paste.

3 Thread 2 scallops onto each of the presoaked skewers. Cover the ends with foil to prevent them burning.

4 Alternate the scallops with the lime segments.

5 Put the oil, lemon juice, salt, and pepper into a bowl and whisk together to make the dressing.

6 Coat the scallops with the spice paste and put over medium-hot coals on a barbecue.

7 Cook for 10 minutes, turning once and basting occasionally.

8 Toss the arugula, mixed salad greens, and dressing together well. transfer to a serving bowl.

9 Serve the scallops piping hot, 2 skewers on each plate immediately with the salad.

asian shellfish kabobs

serves twelve

350 g/12 oz raw jumbo shrimp,
   shelled, leaving tails intact

12 oz/350 g scallops, cleaned,
   trimmed and halved (cut into
   fourths if large)

1 bunch scallions, sliced into
   1-inch/2.5-cm pieces

1 medium red bell pepper,
   seeded and cubed

3½ oz/100 g baby corn cobs,
   trimmed and sliced into
   ½-inch/1-cm pieces

3 tbsp dark soy sauce

½ tsp hot chilli powder

½ tsp ground ginger

1 tbsp corn oil

DIP

4 tbsp dark soy sauce

4 tbsp dry sherry

2 tsp honey

1-inch/2.5-cm piece fresh
   gingerroot, grated

1 scallion, trimmed and sliced
   very finely

1 Soak 12 wooden skewers in
warm water for at least
10 minutes before you use them to
prevent burning. Divide the shrimp,
scallops, scallions, bell pepper, and
baby corn into 12 portions and thread
onto the skewers. Cover the ends with
foil so they do not burn and put into a
shallow dish.

2 Mix the soy sauce, chili powder,
and ground ginger together, and
coat the kabobs. Cover and chill in the
refrigerator for about 2 hours.

3 Arrange the kabobs on a broiler
rack, brush with the oil and cook
under a preheated hot broiler for
2–3 minutes on each side until the
shrimp turn pink, the scallops become
opaque, and the vegetables soften.

4 Mix all the dip ingredients
together in a small bowl.

5 Remove the foil and transfer the
kabobs to a warmed serving
platter and serve with the dip.

lemon angler fish kabobs

serves four

1 lb/450 g angler fish

2 zucchini

1 lemon

12 cherry tomatoes

8 bay leaves

SAUCE

3 tbsp olive oil

2 tbsp lemon juice

1 tsp chopped fresh thyme

½ tsp lemon pepper

salt

TO SERVE

salad greens

crusty bread

VARIATION

Use flounder fillets instead of the angler fish, if you prefer. Allow 2 fillets per person, and skin and cut each fillet lengthwise into 2 pieces. Roll up each piece and thread them onto the skewers.

1 Using a sharp knife, cut the angler fish into 2-inch/5-cm chunks.

2 Cut the zucchini into thick slices and the lemon into wedges.

3 Thread the angler fish, zucchini, lemon, tomatoes, and the bay leaves alternately onto 4 wooden or metal skewers.

4 To make the basting sauce, mix the oil, lemon juice, thyme, lemon pepper, and salt to taste together in a small bowl.

5 Brush the skewers liberally with the basting sauce and put on a barbecue grill. Cook over medium-hot coals for 15 minutes, basting with the sauce, until the fish is cooked through. Transfer to plates and serve with salad greens and bread.

Meat

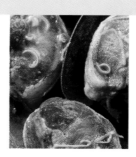

A whole variety of ways in which meat can be cooked is included in this chapter to create a sumptuous selection of dishes. Barbecues, stir-fries, roasts, and casseroles are combined to offer a wealth of textures and flavors. Classic and traditional recipes feature alongside more exotic dishes taken from all around the world, incorporating exciting new ingredients alongside family favorites such as pork and lamb chops. The dishes in this chapter range from easy, economic midweek suppers to sophisticated and elegant main courses for special occasions.

creamed strips of short loin

serves four

6 tbsp butter

1 lb/450 g short loin steak,
    trimmed, and cut into thin strips

6 oz/175 g white mushrooms, sliced

1 tsp mustard

pinch of freshly grated gingerroot

2 tbsp dry sherry

⅔ cup heavy cream

salt and pepper

4 slices hot toast, cut into triangles,
    to serve

PASTA

1 lb/450 g dried rigatoni

2 fresh basil sprigs

½ cup butter

COOK'S TIP

Dried pasta will keep for up to
6 months. Keep it in the package
and reseal it once you have
opened it, or transfer it to an
airtight jar.

1 Melt the butter in a large skillet over a low heat. Add the steak and gently cook, stirring frequently, for 6 minutes. Using a slotted spoon, transfer the steak to an ovenproof dish and keep warm.

2 Add the sliced mushrooms to the skillet and cook for 2–3 minutes in the juices remaining in the skillet. Add the mustard, ginger, salt, and pepper. Cook for 2 minutes, then add the sherry and cream. Cook for an additional 3 minutes, then pour the cream sauce over the steak.

3 Cook the steak and cream sauce mixture in a preheated oven at 375°F/190°C, for 10 minutes.

4 Meanwhile, bring a large pan of lightly salted water to a boil over a medium heat. Add the pasta and 1 of the basil sprigs, and boil rapidly for 10 minutes, or until done. Drain the pasta and transfer to a warmed serving dish. Toss the pasta with the butter and garnish with the other basil sprig.

5 Serve the steak with the pasta and triangles of hot toast.

fresh spaghetti & meatballs

serves four

2½ cups brown bread crumbs

⅝ cup milk

2 tbsp butter

¼ cup whole-wheat flour

⅞ cup beef bouillon

14 oz/400 g canned
    chopped tomatoes

2 tbsp tomato paste

1 tsp sugar

1 tbsp finely chopped fresh tarragon

1 large onion, chopped

4 cups ground steak

1 tsp paprika

4 tbsp olive oil

1 lb/450 g fresh spaghetti

salt and pepper

fresh tarragon sprigs, to garnish

1 Soak the bread crumbs in the milk for 30 minutes.

2 Melt half the butter in a pan over a low heat. Add the flour and cook, stirring, for 2 minutes. Stir in the bouillon and cook for 5 minutes. Add the tomatoes, tomato paste, sugar, and tarragon. Season with salt and pepper and cook for 25 minutes.

3 Mix the onion, steak, and paprika into the bread crumbs and season to taste. Shape into 14 meatballs.

4 Heat the oil and remaining butter in a skillet over a medium heat. Add the meatballs and cook until browned. Put into a deep casserole and pour over the tomato sauce. Cover and cook in a preheated oven at 350°F/180°C, for 25 minutes.

5 Bring a pan of lightly salted water to a boil over a medium heat. Add the pasta and cook until done.

6 Remove the meatballs from the oven and cool slightly. Pile the pasta onto 4 plates, add the meatballs and garnish with tarragon. Serve.

meatballs in italian red wine sauce

serves four

⅔ cup milk

2 cups white bread crumbs

2 tbsp butter

8 tbsp olive oil

3 cups sliced oyster mushrooms

¼ cup whole-wheat flour

⅞ cup beef bouillon

⅔ cup red wine

4 tomatoes, peeled and chopped

1 tbsp tomato paste

1 tsp brown sugar

1 tbsp finely chopped fresh basil

12 shallots, chopped

4 cups ground steak

1 tsp paprika

1 lb/450 g dried egg tagliarini

salt and pepper

fresh basil sprigs, to garnish

1 Soak the bread crumbs in the milk for 30 minutes. Heat half the butter and 4 tablespoons of the oil in a skillet. Add the mushrooms and cook for 4 minutes. Stir in the flour and cook for 2 minutes. Add the bouillon and wine, and cook for 15 minutes. Add the tomatoes, tomato paste, sugar, and basil. Season and cook for 30 minutes.

2 Mix the shallots, steak, and paprika with the breadcrumbs. Season. Shape into 14 meatballs. Heat 4 tablespoons of the remaining oil and butter in a skillet. Fry the meatballs until browned, then put in a casserole with the sauce. Cook in a preheated oven, at 350°F/180°C, for 30 minutes.

3 Bring a pan of salted water to a boil. Add the pasta and cook until done. Drain and transfer to a dish. Spoon the meatballs on top. Garnish with a basil sprig and serve.

citrus pork chops

½ fennel bulb

1 tbsp juniper berries, minced lightly

about 2 tbsp olive oil

finely grated peel of 1 orange

4 pork chops, each about

    5½ oz/150 g

juice of 1 orange

crisp salad, to serve

COOK'S TIP

Juniper berries are most commonly associated with gin, but they are often added to meat dishes in Italy for a delicate citrus flavor. They can be bought dried from most health-food shops and some larger supermarkets.

1 Finely chop the fennel bulb with a sharp knife. Discard the tough outer leaves and feathery fronds.

2 Grind the juniper berries in a mortar and pestle. Mix the juniper berries with the fennel flesh, oil, and orange peel.

3 Using a sharp knife, score a few cuts all over each pork chop.

4 Put the pork chops in a roasting pan or ovenproof dish, the spoon the fennel and juniper mixture over the pork chops.

5 Carefully pour the orange juice over the top of each pork chop. Cover and let marinate in the refrigerator for about 2 hours.

6 Cook the pork chops, under a preheated hot broiler, for about 10–15 minutes, depending on the thickness of the meat, turning, until the meat is tender and cooked through.

7 Transfer the pork chops to 4 large, warmed serving plates and serve immediately with a crisp salad.

pork chops with sage

serves four

2 tbsp flour

1 tbsp chopped fresh sage or 1 tsp
dried sage

4 boneless, lean pork chops,
trimmed of excess fat

2 tbsp olive oil

1 tbsp butter

2 red onions, sliced into rings

1 tbsp lemon juice

2 tsp superfine sugar

4 plum tomatoes, cut into fourths

salt and pepper

salad greens, to serve

1 Mix the flour, sage, and salt and
pepper to taste on a plate. Lightly
dust the pork chops on both sides with
the seasoned flour.

2 Heat the oil and butter in a skillet
over a medium heat. Add the
pork chops and cook for 6–7 minutes
on each side, or until cooked through.
Drain the pork chops and set aside the
pan juices. Keep warm.

3 Toss the onion in the lemon juice
and cook with the sugar and
tomatoes for 5 minutes, or until tender.
Transfer the pork chops to 4 warmed
serving plates and pour over the pan
juices. Serve with the tomato and
onion mixture and salad greens.

pasta & pork in cream sauce

serves four

1 lb/450 g pork tenderloin,
   sliced thinly

4 tbsp olive oil

8 oz/225 g white mushrooms, sliced

⅞ cup Italian Red Wine Sauce
   (see page 135)

1 tbsp lemon juice

pinch of saffron

3 cups dried orecchioni

4 tbsp heavy cream

12 quail eggs

salt

1 Pound the slices of pork between 2 sheets of plastic wrap until wafer thin, then cut into strips.

2 Heat the oil in a large skillet over a medium heat. Add the pork and cook, stirring. for 5 minutes. Add the mushrooms and cook, stirring, for an additional 2 minutes.

3 Pour over the Italian Red Wine Sauce (see page 135), reduce the heat and simmer gently for 20 minutes.

4 Meanwhile, bring a large pan of lightly salted water to a boil over a medium heat. Add the lemon juice, saffron, and pasta and cook for about 8–10 minutes, or until done. Drain the pasta thoroughly and keep warm.

5 Stir the cream into the skillet with the pork and heat for 4 minutes.

6 Bring a pan of water to a boil over a medium heat and cook the eggs for 3 minutes. Cool thoroughly in cold water and remove the shells.

7 Transfer the pasta to a large, warmed serving plate, top with the pork and the sauce, and garnish with the eggs. Serve immediately.

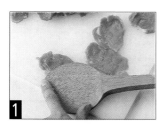

pork with lemon & garlic

serves four

1 lb/450 g pork tenderloin

2½ tbsp chopped almonds

2 tbsp olive oil

3½ oz/100 g prosciutto,
  chopped finely

2 garlic cloves, chopped

1 tbsp fresh oregano, chopped

finely grated peel of 2 lemons

4 shallots, chopped finely

¾ cup ham or chicken bouillon

1 tsp sugar

freshly cooked snow peas, to serve

1 Using a sharp knife, cut the pork into 4 equal pieces. Put the pork between 2 sheets of oiled waxed paper and pound each piece with a meat mallet or the end of a rolling pin to flatten it.

2 Cut a horizontal slit in each piece of pork to make a pocket.

3 Put the almonds onto a cookie sheet and lightly toast under a medium-hot broiler for 2–3 minutes, or until golden.

4 Mix the almonds with 1 tablespoon of the oil, prosciutto, garlic, oregano, and the finely grated peel from 1 lemon. Spoon the mixture into the pork pockets.

5 Heat the remaining oil in a large skillet over a medium heat. Add the shallots and cook for 2 minutes.

6 Add the pork pockets and cook until browned all over.

7 Add the bouillon and bring to a boil over a medium heat. Cook for 45 minutes, or until the meat is tender. Remove the meat and keep warm.

8 Using a zester, pare the remaining lemon. Add the peel and sugar to the skillet, then boil for 3–4 minutes, or until reduced and syrupy. Transfer the pork to 4 warmed serving plates and serve with snow peas.

lamb with olives

serves four

2 lb 12 oz/1.25 kg boned leg
   of lamb

⅓ cup olive oil

2 garlic cloves, minced

1 onion, sliced

1 small fresh red chile, seeded and
   chopped finely

¾ cup dry white wine

1 cup pitted ripe black olives

salt

1 fresh Italian parsley sprig,
   to garnish

1 Using a sharp knife, cut the lamb into 1-inch/2.5-cm cubes.

2 Heat the oil in a skillet over a medium heat. Add the garlic, onion and chile. Cook for 5 minutes.

3 Add the meat and wine, and cook for an additional 5 minutes.

4 Stir in the olives, then transfer the mixture to a casserole. Cook in a preheated oven at 350°F/180°C, for 1 hour 20 minutes, or until the meat is tender. Season with salt to taste. Garnish with a parsley sprig and serve.

roman pan-fried lamb

serves four

1 tbsp oil

1 tbsp butter

1 lb 5 oz/600 g lamb (shoulder or
   leg), cut in 1-inch/2.5-cm chunks

4 garlic cloves, peeled

3 fresh thyme sprigs, stalks removed

6 canned anchovy fillets

²/₃ cup red wine

²/₃ cup lamb or vegetable bouillon

1 tsp sugar

4 tbsp pitted ripe black
   olives, halved

2 tbsp chopped fresh parsley,
   to garnish

COOK'S TIP

Rome is the capital of both the
region of Lazio and Italy and has
thus become a focal point for
specialties from all over Italy.
Food from this region tends to
be simple and quick to prepare,
all with plenty of herbs and
seasonings, giving really
robust flavors.

1 Heat the oil and butter in a large skillet over a medium heat. Add the lamb and cook for 4–5 minutes, stirring, until the meat is browned.

2 Using a mortar and pestle, grind the garlic, thyme, and anchovies together to make a smooth paste.

3 Add the wine and lamb or vegetable bouillon to the skillet. Stir in the garlic and anchovy paste together with the sugar.

4 Bring the mixture to a boil over a medium heat. Reduce the heat, cover and simmer for 30–40 minutes, or until the lamb is tender. For the last 10 minutes of the cooking time, remove the lid to reduce the sauce.

5 Stir the olives into the sauce and mix well.

6 Transfer the lamb and the sauce to a large, warmed serving bowl and garnish with freshly chopped parsley. Serve immediately.

lamb with bay & lemon

serves four

4 lamb chops

1 tbsp oil

1 tbsp butter

⅔ cup white wine

⅔ cup lamb or vegetable bouillon

2 bay leaves

pared peel of 1 lemon

salt and pepper

COOK'S TIP

Your local butcher will offer you good advice on how to prepare the lamb noisettes, if you are wary of preparing them yourself.

1 Using a sharp knife, carefully remove the bone from each lamb chop, keeping the meat intact. Alternatively, ask the butcher to prepare the lamb noisettes for you.

2 Shape the meat into circles and secure with a length of string.

3 Heat the oil and butter together until the mixture starts to froth in a large skillet over a medium heat.

4 Add the lamb noisettes to the skillet and cook for 2–3 minutes on each side, or until the noisettes are browned all over.

5 Remove the skillet from the heat, drain off all the excess fat and discard.

6 Return the skillet to the heat. Add the wine, bouillon, bay leaves and lemon peel and cook for about 20–25 minutes, or until the lamb is tender. Season the lamb noisettes and sauce to taste with salt and pepper.

7 Transfer to 4 large, warmed serving plates. Remove the string from each noisette and serve immediately with the sauce.

barbecued butterfly lamb

serves four

boned leg of lamb, about

4 lb/1.8 kg

8 tbsp balsamic vinegar

grated peel and juice of 1 lemon

⅔ cup corn oil

4 tbsp chopped fresh mint

2 cloves garlic, minced

2 tbsp light brown sugar

salt and pepper

TO SERVE

freshly cooked vegetables

salad greens

1 Open out the boned leg of lamb, so its shape resembles a butterfly. Thread 2–3 skewers through the meat to make it easier to turn on the barbecue grill.

2 Mix the balsamic vinegar, lemon peel and juice, oil, mint, garlic, sugar, and seasoning to taste together in a non-metallic dish large enough to hold the lamb.

3 Put the lamb into the dish and turn until the meat is coated on both sides with the marinade. Let marinate in the refrigerator for at least 6 hours or preferably overnight, turning occasionally.

4 Remove the lamb from the marinade and set aside the liquid for basting.

5 Put the barbecue grill rack about 6 inches/15 cm above the coals on a hot barbecue and grill the lamb for about 30 minutes on each side, turning once and basting frequently with the marinade.

6 Transfer the lamb to a chopping board and remove the skewers. Cut the lamb into slices across the grain and serve with freshly cooked vegetables and salad greens.

lamb chops with rosemary

serves four

8 lamb chops

5 tbsp olive oil

2 tbsp lemon juice

1 clove garlic, chopped finely

½ tsp lemon pepper

salt

8 fresh rosemary sprigs

4 tomatoes, sliced

4 scallions, sliced diagonally

baked potatoes, to serve

DRESSING

2 tbsp olive oil

1 tbsp lemon juice

1 garlic clove, chopped

¼ tsp fresh rosemary, chopped finely

1. Trim the lamb chops by cutting away the flesh with a sharp knife to expose the tips of the bones.

2. Put the oil, lemon juice, garlic, lemon pepper, and salt into a shallow dish and mix with a fork.

3. Lay the rosemary sprigs in the dish and put the lamb on top. Let marinate for at least 1 hour, turning the lamb chops once.

4. Remove the chops from the marinade and wrap foil around the bones to stop them burning.

5. Put the rosemary sprigs on the barbecue rack and put the lamb on top. Grill on a hot barbecue for 10–15 minutes, turning once.

6. Meanwhile make the salad and dressing. Arrange the tomatoes on a serving dish and sprinkle the scallions on top. Put all the ingredients for the dressing in a screw-top jar, shake well and pour over the salad. Serve with the barbecued lamb chops and baked potatoes.

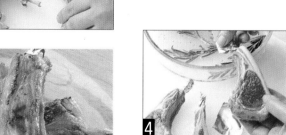

neapolitan veal chops

serves four

¾ cup butter

4 veal chops, 9 oz/250 g
   each, trimmed

1 large onion, sliced

2 apples, peeled, cored, and sliced

6 oz/175 g white mushrooms

1 tbsp chopped fresh tarragon

8 black peppercorns

1 tbsp sesame seeds

14 oz/400 g dried marille

scant ½ cup extra virgin olive oil

2 large beefsteak tomatoes, halved

leaves of 1 fresh basil sprig

¾ cup mascarpone cheese

salt and pepper

1 Melt ¼ cup of the butter in a
skillet over a low heat. Add he
veal and cook for 5 minutes on each
side. Transfer to a dish and keep warm.

2 Add the onion and apples to
the skillet and cook, stirring
frequently, until lightly browned.
Transfer to a serving dish, put the veal
on top and keep warm.

3 Melt the remaining butter in
the skillet over a low heat. Add
the mushrooms, tarragon, and
peppercorns, and cook, stirring
occasionally, for 3 minutes. Sprinkle
over the sesame seeds.

4 Bring a pan of lightly salted water
to a boil over a medium heat.
Add the pasta and 1 teaspoon of the
oil and cook for 8–10 minutes, or until
done. Drain thoroughly and transfer to
an ovenproof dish.

5 Broil or cook the tomatoes and
basil leaves for 2–3 minutes.

6 Top the pasta with the
mascarpone cheese and sprinkle
over the remaining oil. Put the onions,
apples, and veal chops on top of the
pasta, then spoon over the mushrooms,
peppercorns, and pan juices onto the
chops, put the tomatoes and basil
leaves around the edge, and cook in a
preheated oven at 300°F/150°C, for
about 5 minutes.

7 Season to taste with salt and
pepper. Transfer to 4 warmed
serving plates and serve.

vitello tonnato

serves four

1 lb 10 oz/750 g boned leg of
    veal, rolled

2 bay leaves

10 black peppercorns

2–3 cloves

½ tsp salt

2 carrots, sliced

1 onion, sliced

2 celery stalks, sliced

about 3 cups bouillon or water

⅔ cup dry white wine, optional

3 oz/85 g canned tuna, well drained

1½ oz/50 g canned anchovy
    fillets, drained

⅔ cup olive oil

2 tsp canned capers, drained

2 egg yolks

1 tbsp lemon juice

salt and pepper

1 Put the veal in a pan with the bay leaves, peppercorns, cloves, salt, and vegetables. Add enough bouillon and the wine (if using) to barely cover the veal. Bring to a boil over a medium heat, remove any scum from the surface, then cover and simmer gently for about 1 hour, or until tender. Let cool in the water, then drain well.

2 To make the tuna sauce. Mash the tuna with 4 anchovy fillets, 1 tablespoon of oil, and the capers. Add the egg yolks and transfer to a food processor or blender, and process until smooth.

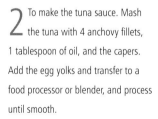

3 Stir in the lemon juice, then gradually whisk in the rest of the oil a few drops at a time until the sauce is smooth and has the consistency of thick cream. Season to taste with salt and pepper.

4 Slice the veal thinly and arrange on a platter. Spoon over the sauce and chill in the refrigerator overnight.

5 Uncover the veal. Arrange the remaining anchovy fillets and the capers in a pattern on top and serve.

veal in a rose petal sauce

serves four

1 lb/450 g dried fettuccine

6 tbsp olive oil

1 tsp chopped fresh oregano

1 tsp chopped fresh marjoram

¾ cup butter

1 lb/450 g veal fillet, sliced thinly

⅔ cup rose petal vinegar
   (see page 106)

⅔ cup fish bouillon

¼ cup grapefruit juice

¼ cup heavy cream

salt

TO GARNISH

12 pink grapefruit segments

12 pink peppercorns

rose petals, washed

fresh herb leaves

1 Bring a large pan of lightly salted water to a boil over a medium heat. Add the pasta and cook for 8–10 minutes, or until done. Drain thoroughly and transfer to a large, warmed serving dish. Sprinkle over 2 tablespoons of the oil, the oregano, and marjoram.

2 Heat 4 tablespoons of the butter with the remaining oil in a large skillet over a low heat. Add the veal and cook for 6 minutes. Remove the veal from the skillet and put on top of the pasta.

3 Add the vinegar and fish bouillon to the skillet and bring to a boil over a medium heat. Boil vigorously until reduced by two thirds. Reduce the heat to low, add the grapefruit juice and cream and simmer for 4 minutes. Dice the remaining butter and add to the skillet, a piece at a time, whisking constantly until it is incorporated.

4 Pour the sauce around the veal, garnish with pink grapefruit segments, pink peppercorns, rose petals, and fresh herb leaves. Serve immediately.

liver with wine sauce

4 slices calf's liver or 8 slices lamb's
   liver, about 1 lb 2 oz/500 g

flour, for coating

1 tbsp olive oil

2 tbsp butter

4½ oz/125 g lean bacon strips,
   derinded and cut into
   narrow strips

1 garlic clove, minced

1 onion, chopped

1 celery stalk, sliced thinly

⅔ cup red wine

⅔ cup beef bouillon

good pinch of ground allspice

1 tsp Worcestershire sauce

1 tsp chopped fresh sage or
   ½ tsp dried sage

3–4 tomatoes, peeled, cut into
   fourths, and·seeded

salt and pepper

fresh sage leaves, to garnish

saute potatoes, to serve

1 Wipe the liver with paper towels, season o taste with salt and pepper, then coat lightly in flour, shaking off any excess.

2 Heat the oil and butter in a skillet over a medium heat. Add the liver and cook until well sealed on both sides and just cooked through. Remove the liver from the skillet, cover and keep warm, but do not let it dry out.

3 Add the bacon to the fat left in the skillet, with the garlic, onion, and celery. Reduce the heat to low and cook gently until soft.

4 Add the red wine, beef bouillon, allspice, Worcestershire sauce, and sage. Season to taste with salt and pepper. Bring to a boil and simmer for 3–4 minutes.

5 Cut each tomato fourth in half. Add to the sauce and continue to cook for 2–3 minutes.

6 Serve the liver on a little of the sauce, with the remainder spooned over. Garnish with fresh sage leaves and serve with saute potatoes.

veal italienne

serves four

5 tbsp butter

1 tbsp olive oil

1½ lb/675 g potatoes, cubed

4 veal escalopes or chops, about
  6 oz/175 g each

1 onion, cut into 8 wedges

2 garlic cloves, minced

2 tbsp all-purpose flour

2 tbsp tomato paste

⅔ cup red wine

1¼ cups chicken bouillon

8 ripe tomatoes, peeled, seeded,
  and diced

2 tbsp pitted ripe black olives, halved

2 tbsp chopped fresh basil

salt and pepper

fresh basil leaves, to garnish

COOK'S TIP

For a quicker cooking time and
really tender meat, pound the
meat with a meat mallet to
flatten it slightly before cooking.

1 Heat the butter and oil in a large skillet over a medium heat. Add the potato cubes and cook for 5–7 minutes, stirring frequently, until they start to brown.

2 Remove the potatoes from the skillet and set aside.

3 Put the veal in the skillet and cook for 2–3 minutes on each side until sealed. Remove from the pan and set aside.

4 Stir the onion and garlic into the skillet and cook for 2–3 minutes.

5 Add the flour and tomato paste and cook for 1 minute, stirring. Gradually blend in the red wine and chicken bouillon, stirring constantly, to make a smooth sauce.

6 Return the potatoes and veal to the skillet. Stir in the tomatoes, olives, and chopped basil. Season to taste with salt and pepper.

7 Transfer to a casserole dish and cook in a preheated oven at 350°F/180°C, for 1 hour, or until the potatoes and veal are cooked through. transfer to 4 warmed serving plates and garnish with basil leaves. Serve.

Chicken & Poultry

For the poultry-lover there are pasta dishes, casseroles, and bakes in this chapter, incorporating a variety of healthy and colorful ingredients. For those who enjoy Italian cuisine there are rich sauces as well as old favorites, such as more traditional casseroles. All these recipes are mouthwatering and quick and easy to prepare. These recipes are also extremely wholesome, offering a comprehensive range of tastes. Those on a low-fat diet should choose lean cuts of meat and look out for lowfat mince to enjoy the dishes featured here.

rich chicken casserole

serves four

8 chicken thighs

2 tbsp olive oil

1 medium red onion, sliced

2 garlic cloves, minced

1 large red bell pepper, sliced thickly

thinly pared peel and juice of
   1 small orange

½ cup chicken bouillon

14 oz/400 g canned
   chopped tomatoes

½ cup sun-dried tomatoes,
   sliced thinly

1 tbsp chopped fresh thyme

½ cup pitted ripe black olives

salt and pepper

TO GARNISH

orange peel

fresh thyme sprigs

crusty fresh bread, to serve

COOK'S TIP

Sun-dried tomatoes have a dense
texture and concentrated taste,
and add intense flavor to
slow-cooking casseroles.

1 In a large heavy-bottomed skillet, cook the chicken without fat over a fairly high heat, turning occasionally until golden brown. Using a slotted spoon, drain off any excess fat from the chicken and transfer to a flameproof casserole dish.

2 Heat the oil in the skillet over a medium heat. Add the onion, garlic, and bell pepper, and cook for 3–4 minutes. Transfer the vegetables to the casserole dish.

3 Add the orange peel and juice, chicken bouillon, chopped tomatoes, and sun-dried tomatoes to the casserole and stir well.

4 Bring to a boil, then cover the casserole with a lid and simmer very gently over a low heat for about 1 hour, stirring occasionally. Add the chopped thyme and black olives, then season to taste with salt and pepper.

5 Spoon the chicken casserole onto 4 warmed serving plates, garnish with orange peel and thyme, and serve with crusty bread.

garlic & herb chicken

serves four

4 chicken breasts, skin removed

⅓ cup full-fat soft cheese, flavored
with herbs and garlic

8 slices prosciutto

⅔ cup red wine

⅔ cup chicken bouillon

1 tbsp brown sugar

salad greens, to serve

1 Using a sharp knife, make a horizontal slit along the length of each chicken breast to form a pocket.

2 Put the cheese into a bowl and beat with a wooden spoon to soften it. Spoon the cheese into the pocket of the chicken breasts.

3 Wrap 2 slices of prosciutto around each chicken breast and secure in with a length of string.

4 Pour the wine and chicken bouillon into a large skillet and bring to a boil over a medium heat. When the mixture is just starting to boil, add the sugar and stir to dissolve.

5 Add the chicken breasts to the mixture in the skillet. Simmer for 12–15 minutes, or until the chicken is tender and the juices run clear when the point of a sharp knife is inserted into the thickest part of the meat.

6 Remove the chicken from the skillet, set aside and keep warm.

7 Heat the sauce and boil until reduced and thickened. Remove the string from the chicken and cut into slices. Pour the sauce over the chicken and serve with salad greens.

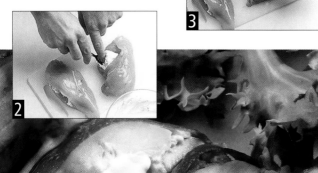

VARIATION

Try adding 2 finely chopped sun-dried tomatoes to the soft cheese in step 2, if you wish.

chicken pepperonata

serves four

8 skinless chicken thighs

2 tbsp whole-wheat flour

2 tbsp olive oil

1 small onion, sliced thinly

1 garlic clove, minced

1 each large red, yellow, and green

    bell peppers, sliced thinly

14 oz/400 g canned

    chopped tomatoes

1 tbsp chopped fresh oregano

salt and pepper

fresh oregano leaves, to garnish

COOK'S TIP

If you do not have fresh oregano,
use canned tomatoes with herbs
already added.

1 Remove the skin from the chicken thighs and toss in the flour.

2 Heat the oil in a pan over a high heat. Add the chicken and cook until browned. Remove from the pan. Add the onion and cook until soft. Add the garlic, peppers, tomatoes, and oregano, then bring to a boil.

3 Arrange the chicken over the vegetables. Season well with salt and pepper, then cover and simmer for 20–25 minutes, or until the chicken is tender and the juices run clear when the point of a sharp knife is inserted into the thickest part of the meat.

4 Season to taste, then transfer the chicken to a large dish and garnish with oregano. Serve.

chicken with orange sauce

serves four

2 tbsp canola oil

2 tbsp olive oil

4 x 8 oz/225 g chicken breasts

⅔ cup brandy

2 tbsp all-purpose flour

⅔ cup freshly squeezed
orange juice

1 oz/25 g zucchini, cut into
thin batons

1 oz/25 g red bell pepper, cut into
thin batons

1 oz/25 g leek, shredded finely

14 oz/400 g dried
whole-wheat spaghetti

3 large oranges, peeled and cut
into segments

peel of 1 orange, cut into very
fine strips

2 tbsp chopped fresh tarragon

⅔ cup ricotta cheese

salt and pepper

1 Heat the canola oil and 1 tablespoon of the olive oil in a large skillet over a fairly high heat. Add the chicken and cook until golden brown. Add the brandy and cook for about 3 minutes. Sprinkle in the flour and cook, stirring constantly, for about 2 minutes.

2 Reduce the heat and add the orange juice, zucchini, red bell pepper, and leek. Season to taste with salt and pepper. Simmer for 5 minutes until the sauce has thickened.

3 Meanwhile, bring a pan of lightly salted water to a boil over a medium heat. Add the pasta and cook for 10 minutes, or until done. Drain the pasta thoroughly and transfer to a warmed serving dish. Drizzle over the remaining oil.

4 Add half the orange segments, half the orange peel, the chopped tarragon, and ricotta cheese to the sauce in the skillet and cook for about 3 minutes.

5 Put the chicken on top of the pasta, pour over a little sauce, garnish with the remaining orange segments, peel, and tarragon. Serve immediately with any extra sauce.

rolled chicken slices with mortadella

serves four

1 chicken, weighing about
5 lb/2.25 kg

8 slices mortadella or salami

2 cups fresh white or brown
bread crumbs

1 cup freshly grated
Parmesan cheese

2 garlic cloves, minced

6 tbsp chopped fresh basil
or parsley

1 egg, beaten

pepper

fresh spring vegetables, to serve

VARIATION
Replace the mortadella with
strips of lean bacon,
if you prefer.

1 Bone the chicken, keeping the skin intact. Dislocate each leg by breaking it at the thigh joint. Cut down each side of the backbone, taking care not to pierce the breast skin.

2 Pull the backbone clear of the flesh and discard. Remove the ribs, carefully severing any attached flesh with a sharp knife.

3 Scrape the flesh from each leg and cut away the bone at the joint with a knife or shears.

4 Use the bones for bouillon. Lay out the boned chicken on a board, skin-side down. Arrange the mortadella slices over the chicken, overlapping slightly.

5 Put the bread crumbs, Parmesan cheese, garlic, and basil into a bowl. Season with pepper and mix, then stir in the beaten egg. Pile the mixture down the center of the boned chicken, then roll the meat around it and tie securely with fine cotton string.

6 Put into a roasting pan and brush with oil. Roast in a preheated oven at 400°F/200°C, for 1½ hours, or until the chicken is tender and the juices run clear when the point of a sharp knife is inserted into the thickest part of the meat.

7 Serve hot or cold, in slices, with fresh spring vegetables.

mustard-baked chicken

serves four

8 chicken portions, 4 oz/115 g each

4 tbsp butter, melted

4 tbsp mild mustard (see Cook's Tip)

2 tbsp lemon juice

1 tbsp brown sugar

1 tsp paprika

3 tbsp poppy seeds

3½ cups dried pasta shells

1 tsp olive oil

salt and pepper

COOK'S TIP

Dijon is the type of mustard most often used in cooking, as it has a clean and only mildly spicy flavor. German mustard has a sweet-sour taste, with Bavarian mustard being slightly sweeter. American mustard is mild and sweet.

1 Arrange the chicken portions in a single layer in a large oven-proof dish.

2 Mix the butter, mustard, lemon juice, sugar, and paprika together in a bowl and season to taste with salt and pepper. Brush the mixture over the upper surfaces of the chicken portions and cook in a preheated oven at 400°F/200°C, for 15 minutes.

3 Remove the dish from the oven and carefully turn over the chicken portions. Coat the upper surfaces of the chicken with the remaining mustard mixture, sprinkle the chicken portions with poppy seeds. Return to the oven for an additional 15 minutes.

4 Meanwhile, bring a large pan of lightly salted water to a boil over a medium heat. Add the pasta shells and oil and cook for 8–10 minutes, or until done.

5 Drain the pasta thoroughly and transfer to 4 warmed serving plates. Top the pasta with 1 or 2 of the chicken portions, pour over the mustard sauce and serve immediately.

chicken with green olives

serves four

3 tbsp olive oil

2 tbsp butter

4 part boned chicken breasts

1 large onion, chopped finely

2 garlic cloves, minced

2 red, yellow, or green bell peppers,
   seeded and cut into large pieces

9 oz/250 g white mushrooms, sliced
   or cut into fourths

6 oz/175 g tomatoes, peeled
   and halved

⅔ cup dry white wine

1½ cups pitted green olives

4–6 tbsp heavy cream

14 oz/400 g dried pasta

salt and pepper

chopped fresh Italian parsley,
   to garnish

1 Heat 2 tablespoons of the oil and the butter in a skillet over a medium heat. Add the chicken breasts and cook until golden brown all over. Remove the chicken from the skillet.

2 Add the onion and garlic to the skillet and cook until starting to soften. Add the bell peppers and mushrooms, and cook for 2–3 minutes.

3 Add the tomatoes and season to taste with salt and pepper. Transfer the vegetables to a casserole dish and arrange the chicken on top.

4 Add the wine to the skillet and bring to a boil over a medium heat. Pour the wine over the chicken. Cover and cook in a preheated oven at 350°F/180°C, for 50 minutes.

5 Add the olives to the casserole and stir well. Pour in the cream, cover, and return to the oven for an additional 10–20 minutes.

6 Meanwhile, bring a large pan of lightly salted water to a boil over a medium heat. Add the pasta and the remaining oil and cook for about 8–10 minutes, or until done. Drain the pasta thoroughly and keep warm.

7 Remove the chicken from the oven and garnish with the chopped parsley. Transfer the pasta to a warmed serving plate and serve the chicken straight from the casserole. Alternatively, transfer the pasta to a warmed serving dish, put the chicken on top, spoon over the sauce, and garnish with the parsley. Serve.

chicken marengo

serves four

8 chicken portions

1 tbsp olive oil

10½ oz/300 g strained tomatoes

¾ cup white wine

2 tsp dried mixed herbs

3 tbsp butter, melted

2 garlic cloves, minced

8 slices white bread

3½ oz/100 g mixed mushrooms
(such as white, oyster, and cèpes)

⅓ cup ripe black olives, chopped

1 tsp sugar

fresh basil leaves, to garnish

COOK'S TIP

If you have time, marinate
the chicken portions in the wine
and herbs and chill in the
refrigerator for 2 hours. This will
make the chicken more tender
and accentuate the wine flavor
of the sauce.

1 Remove the bone from each of the chicken portions, using a sharp knife.

2 Heat the oil in a large skillet over a medium heat. Add the chicken portions and cook for 4–5 minutes, turning occasionally, or until browned.

3 Add the tomato paste, wine, and mixed herbs to the skillet. Bring to a boil over a medium heat, then cook for 30 minutes, or until the chicken is tender and the juices run clear when the point of a sharp knife is inserted into the thickest part of the meat.

4 Mix the melted butter and garlic together in a small bowl. Lightly toast the slices of bread and brush with the garlic butter. Keep warm.

5 Heat the remaining oil in a separate skillet over a low heat. Add the mushrooms and cook for 2–3 minutes, or until just brown.

6 Add the olives and sugar to the chicken mixture and cook until warmed through.

7 Transfer the chicken and sauce to 4 warmed serving plates. Garnish with basil leaves and serve with the bruschetta, and cooked mushrooms.

chicken cacciatora

serves four

1 roasting chicken, about
   3 lb 5 oz/1.5 kg, cut into
   6–8 serving pieces
1 cup all-purpose flour
3 tbsp olive oil
⅔ cup dry white wine
1 green bell pepper, seeded
   and sliced
1 red bell pepper, seeded and sliced
1 carrot, chopped finely
1 celery stalk, chopped finely
1 garlic clove, minced
7 oz/200 g canned
   chopped tomatoes
salt and pepper

1 Rinse the chicken pieces and pat dry with paper towels. Mix the flour and salt and pepper to taste on a plate, then lightly dust the chicken with seasoned flour.

2 Heat the oil in a large skillet over a medium heat. Add the chicken and cook until browned. Remove from the skillet and set aside.

3 Drain off all but 2 tablespoons of the fat in the skillet. Add the wine and stir for a few minutes. Add the bell peppers, carrots, celery, and garlic. Season to taste with salt and pepper and simmer for about 15 minutes.

4 Add the chopped tomatoes to the skillet. Cover and simmer for 30 minutes, stirring often, until the chicken is completely cooked through.

5 Transfer the chicken and sauce to 4 warmed plates and serve.

broiled chicken

serves four

8 part-boned chicken thighs

1 tbsp olive oil for brushing

1⅔ cups strained tomatoes

½ cup green or red pesto sauce
   (store bought)

12 slices French bread

1 cup freshly grated
   Parmesan cheese

½ cup pine nuts or slivered almonds

assorted salad greens, to serve

COOK'S TIP

Although leaving the skin on the chicken means that it will have a higher fat content, many people like the rich taste and crispy skin, especially when it is blackened by the grill. The skin also keeps in the cooking juices.

1 Arrange the chicken thighs in a single layer in a wide flameproof dish and brush lightly with oil. Cook under a preheated hot broiler for about 15 minutes, turning occasionally, until golden brown.

2 Insert the point of a sharp knife into the thickest part of the meat to ensure that there is no trace of pink in the juices.

3 Pour off any excess fat. Warm the strained tomatoes and half the pesto sauce in a small pan and pour over the chicken. Broil for a few more minutes, turning until coated.

4 Spread the remaining pesto onto the bread and arrange over the chicken and sprinkle with Parmesan cheese. Sprinkle the pine nuts over the cheese. Broil until browned and bubbling. Serve with salad greens.

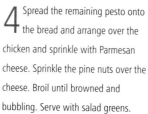

italian chicken spirals

serves four

4 skinless, boneless chicken breasts

1 cup fresh basil leaves

2 tbsp hazelnuts

1 garlic clove, minced

2 cups whole-wheat pasta spirals

2 sun-dried tomatoes or
    fresh tomatoes

1 tbsp lemon juice

1 tbsp olive oil

1 tbsp capers

½ cup ripe black olives

salt and pepper

VARIATION
Sun-dried tomatoes have a
wonderful, rich flavor; but if
you can't find them, use
fresh tomatoes instead.

1 Beat a chicken breast between
2 sheets of plastic wrap with a
rolling pin to flatten evenly. Repeat
with the remaining chicken breasts.

2 Put the basil and hazelnuts into a
food processor and process until
finely chopped. Mix with the garlic and
season to taste with salt and pepper.

3 Spread the basil mixture over the
chicken and roll up from a short
end to enclose. Wrap in foil and seal.

4 Bring a pan of lightly salted water
to a boil over a medium heat.
Add the pasta and cook until done.

5 Put the chicken parcels into a
steamer basket or strainer set
over the pan. Cover and steam for
10 minutes. Dice the tomatoes.

6 Drain the pasta and return to the
pan with the lemon juice, oil,
tomatoes, capers, and olives. Heat.

7 Insert the point of a sharp knife
into the chicken to make sure the
juices run clear, then slice. Transfer the
pasta to a large serving dish and put
the chicken on top, then serve.

chicken spirals

serves four

4 skinless, boneless chicken breasts

1 garlic clove, minced

2 tbsp tomato paste

4 slices smoked lean bacon

large handful of fresh basil leaves

2 tbsp vegetable oil for brushing

salt and pepper

salad greens, to serve

1 Spread out a chicken breast between 2 sheets of plastic wrap and beat firmly with a rolling pin or meat mallet to flatten the chicken to an even thickness. Repeat with the remaining chicken portions.

2 Mix the garlic and tomato paste together and spread the mixture over the chicken. Lay a bacon slice over each, then sprinkle with the basil. Season to taste with salt and pepper.

3 Roll up each piece of chicken firmly, then cut into thick slices. Thread the slices onto 4 skewers, making sure the skewer holds the chicken in a spiral shape.

4 Brush lightly with oil and cook on a hot barbecue or under a preheated hot broiler for 10 minutes, turning once. Serve immediately with salad greens.

pesto-baked partridge

serves four

8 partridge pieces, 115 g/4 oz each

4 tbsp butter, melted

4 tbsp Dijon mustard

2 tbsp lime juice

1 tbsp brown sugar

6 tbsp Pesto Sauce (see page 227)

1 lb/450 g dried rigatoni

1 tsp olive oil

1 cup freshly grated
   Parmesan cheese

salt and pepper

VARIATION
You could also prepare
young pheasant in the
same way.

1 Arrange the partridge pieces,
smooth-side down, in a single
layer in a large ovenproof dish.

2 Mix the butter, Dijon mustard,
lime juice, and brown sugar
together in a small bowl. Season to
taste with salt and pepper, then brush
this mixture over the partridge pieces
and cook in a preheated oven at
400°F/200°C, for 15 minutes.

3 Remove the dish from the oven
and coat the partridge with
3 tablespoons of the Pesto Sauce (see
page 227). Return to the oven and
cook for an additional 12 minutes.

4 Remove the dish from the oven
and turn the partridge over. Coat
with the remaining mustard mixture
and return to the oven for 10 minutes.

5 Meanwhile, bring a large pan of
lightly salted water to a boil over
a medium heat. Add the pasta and oil
and cook for 8–10 minutes, or until
done. Drain and transfer to a serving
dish. Toss the pasta with the remaining
Pesto Sauce and Parmesan cheese.
Serve the partridge with the pasta,
pouring over the cooking juices.

slices of duck with pasta

serves four

4 x 9 oz/250 g boneless
  duck breasts

2 tbsp butter

⅓ cup finely chopped carrots

4 tbsp finely chopped shallots

1 tbsp lemon juice

⅔ cup meat bouillon

4 tbsp honey

⅔ cup fresh or thawed
  frozen raspberries

¼ cup all-purpose flour

1 tbsp Worcestershire sauce

14 oz/400 g dried linguine

salt and pepper

TO GARNISH

fresh raspberries

fresh Italian parsley sprigs

1 Trim and score the duck breasts with a sharp knife and season to taste with salt and pepper. Melt the butter in a skillet over a medium heat. Add the duck breasts, and cook until lightly colored.

2 Add the carrots, shallots, lemon juice, and half the bouillon and simmer over a low heat for 1 minute. Stir in half the honey and half the raspberries. Sprinkle over half the flour and cook, stirring constantly, for 3 minutes. Season with pepper to taste and add the Worcestershire sauce.

3 Stir in the remaining bouillon and cook for 1 minute. Stir in the remaining honey and remaining raspberries and sprinkle over the remaining flour. Cook for an additional 3 minutes.

4 Remove the duck breasts from the skillet, but leave the sauce to continue simmering over a very low heat.

5 Meanwhile, bring a large pan of lightly salted water to a boil over a medium heat. Add the pasta and cook for 8–10 minutes, or until done. Drain and transfer to 4 large, warmed serving plates.

6 Slice the duck breast lengthwise into ¼-inch/5-mm thick pieces. Pour a little sauce over the pasta and arrange the sliced duck in a fan shape on top of it. Garnish with raspberries and parsley sprigs, then serve.

Pasta & Rice

Pasta and rice are quick and easy to cook and, when combined with a variety of ingredients, can produce an enormous variety of dishes.

To cook pasta, bring a pan of lightly salted water to a boil over a medium heat. Add the pasta and 1 teaspoon of olive oil. Do not cover, but bring the water to a rolling boil. When the pasta is tender, but firm to the bite, drain thoroughly and toss with butter, olive oil, or a sauce of your choice. As a rough guide, fresh unfilled pasta will take three minutes, filled fresh pasta will take 10 minutes to cook. Dried pasta will take approximately 10–15 minutes. To cook a good quality rice like basmati, soak it for about 20–30 minutes to prevent the grains from sticking to each other. Add it to gently boiling, lightly salted water, stir once and cook until tender, but firm to the bite. This will take up to 20 minutes.

sicilian spaghetti cake

serves four

⅝ cup olive oil, plus extra
   for brushing

2 eggplant

3 cups ground beef

1 onion, chopped

2 garlic cloves, minced

2 tbsp tomato paste

14 oz/400 g canned
   chopped tomatoes

1 tsp Worcestershire sauce

1 tsp chopped fresh marjoram or
   oregano or ½ tsp dried marjoram
   or oregano

½ cup pitted ripe black olives, sliced

1 green, red, or yellow bell pepper,
   cored, seeded, and chopped

6 oz/175 g dried spaghetti

1 cup freshly grated
   Parmesan cheese

salt and pepper

1 Brush an 8 inch loose-based round cake pan with oil. Line the base with baking parchment and brush with oil.

2 Slice the eggplant. Heat a little oil in a pan over a medium heat. Add the eggplant and cook, in batches, until browned on both sides. Add more oil, as necessary. Drain on paper towels.

3 Put the beef, onion, and garlic in a pan and cook over a medium heat, stirring, until browned. Add the tomato paste, tomatoes, Worcestershire sauce, marjoram or oregano, and salt and pepper. Simmer, stirring, for 10 minutes. Add the olives and bell pepper, and cook for 10 minutes.

4 Bring a pan of salted water to a boil over a medium heat. Add the pasta and cook until just done. Drain the pasta and transfer to a large bowl. Add the meat mixture and cheese and toss with 2 forks.

5 Arrange the eggplant slices over the bottom and up the sides of the pan. Add the pasta and cover with the rest of the eggplant slices. Cook in a preheated oven at 400°F/200°C, for 40 minutes. Let stand for 5 minutes, then invert onto a large serving dish. Discard the baking parchment and serve immediately.

pasticcio

serves six

2 cups fusilli, or other short
   pasta shapes

1 tsp olive oil

4 tbsp heavy cream

salt

fresh rosemary sprigs, to garnish

MEAT SAUCE

2 tbsp olive oil, plus extra
   for brushing

1 onion, sliced thinly

1 red bell pepper, seeded
   and chopped

2 garlic cloves, chopped

1 lb 6 oz/625 g lean ground beef

14 oz/400 g canned
   chopped tomatoes

½ cup dry white wine

2 tbsp chopped fresh parsley

1¾ oz/50 g canned anchovy fillets,
   drained and chopped

salt and pepper

TOPPING

1¼ cups plain yogurt

3 eggs

pinch of freshly grated nutmeg

⅔ cup freshly grated
   Parmesan cheese

1 To make the sauce, heat the oil in a large skillet over a medium heat. Add the onion and bell pepper and cook for 3 minutes. Stir in the garlic and cook for 1 minute. Add the beef and cook, stirring, until browned.

2 Add the tomatoes and wine, stir well, and bring to a boil over a medium heat. Simmer for 20 minutes, or until the sauce is fairly thick. Stir in the parsley and anchovies. Season to taste with salt and pepper.

3 Bring a large pan of lightly salted water to a boil over a medium heat. Add the pasta and oil and cook for 8–10 minutes, or until just done. Drain, then transfer to a bowl. Stir in the cream and set aside.

4 To make the topping, beat the yogurt with the eggs and nutmeg until well mixed and season to taste.

5 Brush a large shallow casserole with oil. Spoon in half the pasta mixture and cover with half the meat sauce. Repeat these layers, then spread the topping over the final layer. Sprinkle the Parmesan cheese on top.

6 Cook in a preheated oven at 375°F/190°C, for 25 minutes, or until the topping is golden brown and bubbling. Garnish with rosemary sprigs and serve immediately.

spaghetti bolognese

serves four

1 tbsp olive oil

1 onion, chopped finely

2 garlic cloves, chopped

1 carrot, scraped and chopped

1 celery stalk, chopped

1¾ oz/50 g pancetta or lean
   bacon, diced

1½ cups lean minced beef

400 g/14 oz canned tomatoes

2 tsp dried oregano

scant ½ cup red wine

2 tbsp tomato paste

1 lb 7 oz/650 g fresh spaghetti or
   12 oz/350 g dried spaghetti

salt and pepper

VARIATION
Try adding 25 g/1 oz dried
porcini, soaked for 10 minutes
in 2 tablespoons of warm water,
to the bolognese sauce in
step 4, if you wish.

1 Heat the oil in a large skillet over a medium heat. Add the onions and cook for 3 minutes.

2 Add the garlic, carrot, celery, and pancetta or bacon and cook over a fairly high heat for 3–4 minutes, or until just starting to brown.

3 Add the beef and cook over a high heat for 3 minutes, or until the meat has browned.

4 Stir in the tomatoes, oregano, and red wine . Bring to a boil over a medium heat. Reduce the heat and simmer for about 45 minutes.

5 Stir in the tomato paste and season with salt and pepper.

6 Bring a large pan of lightly salted water to a boil over a medium heat. Add the pasta and cook for about 8–10 minutes, or until just done. Drain the pasta thoroughly.

7 Transfer the pasta to a large serving plate and pour over the bolognese sauce. Toss with 2 forks to mix and serve immediately.

tagliatelle & chicken sauce

serves four

Tomato Sauce (see page 187)

8 oz/225 g fresh or dried
    green tagliatelle

salt

fresh basil leaves, to garnish

CHICKEN SAUCE

4 tbsp sweet butter

14 oz/400 g skinless, boneless
    chicken breast portions,
    sliced thinly

¾ cup blanched almonds

1¼ cups heavy cream

salt and pepper

1 Make the Tomato Sauce (see page 187), set aside, and keep warm.

2 To make the chicken sauce, melt the butter in a large, heavy-bottomed skillet over a medium heat. Add the chicken strips and almonds and cook, stirring frequently, for about 5–6 minutes, or until the chicken is cooked through.

3 Meanwhile, pour the cream into a small pan, set over a low heat, and bring to a boil. Boil for 10 minutes until reduced by almost half. Pour the cream over the chicken and almonds, stir well, and season to taste with salt and pepper. Remove the pan from the heat, set aside, and keep warm.

4 Bring a large pan of lightly salted water to a boil over a medium heat. Add the pasta and cook until just done. Fresh tagliatelle will take about 2–3 minutes and dried pasta will take 8–10 minutes. Drain, return to the pan, cover, and keep warm.

5 When ready to serve, turn the pasta into a warmed serving dish and spoon the tomato sauce over it. Spoon the chicken and cream into the center, sprinkle with fresh basil leaves, and serve immediately.

tagliatelle & meatballs

serves four

1 lb 2 oz/500 g ground lean beef

1 cup soft white bread crumbs

1 garlic clove, minced

2 tbsp chopped fresh parsley

1 tsp dried oregano

pinch of freshly grated nutmeg

¼ tsp ground coriander

⅔ cup freshly grated
   Parmesan cheese

2–3 tbsp milk

all-purpose flour, for dusting

3 tbsp olive oil

14 oz/400 g dried tagliatelle

2 tbsp butter, diced

salt and pepper

SAUCE

3 tbsp olive oil

2 large onions, sliced

2 celery stalks, sliced thinly

2 garlic cloves, chopped

14 oz/400 g canned
   chopped tomatoes

4½ oz/125 g sun-dried tomatoes in
   oil, drained and chopped

2 tbsp tomato paste

1 tbsp molasses sugar

⅔ cup white wine or water

1 To make the tomato sauce, heat the oil in a skillet over a medium heat. Add the onions and celery, and cook until translucent. Add the garlic and cook for 1 minute. Stir in the tomatoes, tomato paste, sugar, and wine, and season to taste. Bring to a boil and cook for 10 minutes.

2 Break up the meat in a bowl with a wooden spoon until it becomes a sticky paste. Stir in the bread crumbs, garlic, herbs, and spices. Stir in the cheese and enough milk to make a firm paste. Flour your hands, take spoonfuls of the mixture, and shape into 12 balls. Heat the oil in a skillet over a high heat. Add the meatballs and cook for 5–6 minutes, or until browned.

3 Pour the tomato sauce over the meatballs. Reduce the heat, cover, and simmer for 30 minutes, turning once or twice.

4 Bring a large pan of lightly salted water to a boil over a medium heat. Add the pasta and cook for 8–10 minutes, or until just done. Drain the pasta thoroughly, then transfer to a warmed serving dish, dot with the butter, and toss with 2 forks. Spoon the meatballs and sauce over the pasta and serve immediately.

187

spaghetti with ricotta cheese sauce

serves four

12 oz/350 g dried spaghetti

3 tbsp butter

2 tbsp chopped fresh Italian parsley

1 tbsp pine nuts

salt and pepper

1 fresh Italian parsley sprig,
   to garnish

SAUCE

1 cup freshly ground almonds

½ cup ricotta cheese

pinch of freshly grated nutmeg

pinch of ground cinnamon

⅔ cup sour cream

2 tbsp olive oil

½ cup hot chicken bouillon

1 Bring a pan of lightly salted water to a boil over a medium heat. Add the pasta and cook for about 8–10 minutes, or until just done.

2 Drain the pasta, return to the pan, and toss with the butter and parsley. Set aside and keep warm.

3 To make the sauce, mix the ground almonds, ricotta cheese, nutmeg, cinnamon, and sour cream in a small pan and stir over a low heat to a thick paste. Gradually stir in the oil. When the oil has been incorporated, gradually stir in the hot chicken bouillon, until smooth. Season with pepper to taste.

4 Transfer the pasta to a warmed serving dish, pour the sauce over, and toss together well (see Cook's Tip). Sprinkle over the pine nuts, garnish with the an Italian parsley sprig parsley, and serve immediately.

COOK'S TIP

It is best to use 2 large forks to toss the cooked spaghetti or other long pasta, to make sure that the pasta is thoroughly coated with the sauce. You can also purchase specially designed spaghetti forks, which are available from some cookware departments and large kitchen stores.

penne & butternut squash

serves four

2 tbsp olive oil

1 garlic clove, minced

1 cup fresh white bread crumbs

1 lb 2 oz/500 g butternut squash,
    peeled and seeded

8 tbsp water

1 lb 2 oz/500 g fresh penne, or
    other pasta shapes

1 tbsp butter

1 onion, sliced

4 oz/115 g ham, cut into strips

scant 1 cup light cream

½ cup freshly grated cheddar cheese

2 tbsp chopped fresh parsley

salt and pepper

1 Mix the oil, garlic, and bread crumbs together and spread out on a large plate. Cook in the microwave on HIGH for 4–5 minutes, stirring every minute, until crisp and starting to brown. Remove from the microwave and set aside.

2 Dice the squash. Put into a large bowl with half the water. Cover and cook on HIGH for 8–9 minutes, stirring occasionally. Let stand for 2 minutes.

3 Put the pasta into a large bowl, add a little salt, and pour over boiling water to cover by 1 inch/ 2.5 cm. Cover and cook on HIGH for 5 minutes, stirring once, until the pasta is just done. Let stand, covered, for 1 minute before draining.

4 Put the butter and onion into a large bowl. Cover and cook on HIGH for 3 minutes.

5 Coarsely mash the squash, using a fork. Add to the onion with the pasta, ham, cream, cheese, parsley, and remaining water. Season to taste and mix well. Cover and cook on HIGH for 4 minutes until heated through.

6 Transfer the pasta to a large, warmed serving plate, sprinkle with the crisp garlic crumbs and serve.

spaghetti olio e aglio

serves four

½ cup olive oil

3 garlic cloves, minced

1 lb.450 g fresh spaghetti

3 tbsp coarsely chopped
    fresh parsley

salt and pepper

COOK'S TIP

Oils produced by different countries—mainly Italy, Spain, and Greece—have their own characteristic flavors. Some produce an oil that has a hot, peppery taste while others have a "green" flavor.

2 Meanwhile, bring a large pan of lightly salted water to a boil over a medium heat. Add the pasta and remaining oil, and cook for about 2–3 minutes, or until just done. Drain the thoroughly and return to the pan.

1 Reserve 1 teaspoon of the oil and heat the remainder in a pan over a low heat. Add the garlic and a pinch of salt, and cook, stirring constantly, until golden brown, then remove the pan from the heat. Do not let the garlic burn as this will taint the flavor of the oil. (If it does burn, you will have to start all over again!)

3 Add the oil and garlic mixture to the pasta and toss to coat thoroughly. Season with pepper to taste, then add the chopped parsley and toss to coat again.

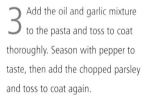

4 Transfer the pasta to a warmed serving dish and serve.

191

pasta with green vegetables

serves four

2 cups dried gemelli or other
    pasta shapes
1 broccoli head, cut into flowerets
2 zucchini, sliced
8 oz/225 g asparagus spears
4 oz/115 g snow peas
1 cup frozen peas
2 tbsp butter
3 tbsp vegetable bouillon
4 tbsp heavy cream
freshly grated nutmeg
2 tbsp chopped fresh parsley
2 tbsp freshly grated
    Parmesan cheese
salt and pepper

1 Bring a large pan of lightly salted water to a boil over a medium heat. Add the pasta and cook for 8–10 minutes, or until just done. Drain the pasta thoroughly, return to the pan, cover, and keep warm.

2 Put the broccoli, zucchini, asparagus spears, and snow peas into a steamer basket set over a pan of boiling salted water until they are just starting to soften. Remove from the heat and refresh in cold water. Drain and set aside.

3 Bring a small pan of lightly salted water to a boil over a medium heat. Add the frozen peas and cook for 3 minutes. Drain the peas, refresh in cold water, and then drain again. Set aside with the other vegetables.

4 Put the butter and vegetable bouillon in a pan over a medium heat. Add the vegetables, setting aside a few of the asparagus spears, and toss carefully with a wooden spoon until they have heated through, taking care not to break them up.

5 Stir in the cream and heat through without bringing to a boil. Season to taste with salt, pepper, and nutmeg.

6 Transfer the pasta to a large, warmed serving dish and stir in the chopped parsley. Spoon over the vegetable sauce and sprinkle over the Parmesan cheese. Arrange the reserved asparagus spears in a decorative pattern on top and serve.

pasta with cheese & broccoli

serves four

10½ oz/300 g dried tricolor
   tagliatelle (plain, spinach- and
   tomato-flavored noodles)
2½ cups broccoli, broken into
   small flowerets
1½ cups mascarpone cheese
1 cup blue cheese, chopped
1 tbsp chopped fresh oregano
2 tbsp butter
salt and pepper
fresh oregano sprigs, to garnish
freshly grated Parmesan cheese,
   to serve

1 Bring a large pan of lightly salted water to a boil over a medium heat. Add the pasta and cook for 8–10 minutes, or until just done.

2 Meanwhile, cook the broccoli in a small amount of lightly salted, boiling water. Avoid overcooking, so it retains much of its color and texture.

3 Heat the mascarpone and blue cheeses together gently in a pan over a low heat until they are melted. Stir in the oregano and season to taste with salt and pepper.

4 Drain the pasta thoroughly. Return it to the pan. Add the butter, and, using 2 forks, toss the pasta to coat it thoroughly. Drain the broccoli and add to the pasta with the sauce, tossing gently to mix.

5 Transfer the pasta to 4 large, warmed serving plates. Garnish with oregano sprigs and serve with Parmesan cheese.

pasta & vegetable sauce

serves four

3 tbsp olive oil

1 onion, sliced

2 garlic cloves, chopped

3 red bell peppers, seeded and
cut into strips

3 zucchini, sliced

14 oz/400 g canned
chopped tomatoes

3 tbsp sun-dried tomato paste

2 tbsp chopped fresh basil

2 cups fresh fusilli

1 cup freshly grated Swiss cheese

salt and pepper

4 fresh basil sprigs, to garnish

1 Heat the oil in a large pan or casserole dish. Add the onion and garlic and cook, stirring occasionally, until softened. Add the bell peppers and zucchini, and cook, stirring occasionally, for 5 minutes.

2 Add the tomatoes, sun-dried tomato paste, and basil, and season to taste with salt and pepper. Cover and cook for 5 minutes.

3 Meanwhile, bring a large pan of salted water to a boil over a medium heat. Add the pasta and cook for 3 minutes, or until just tender. Drain the pasta thoroughly and add to the vegetable mixture. Toss gently to mix .

4 Transfer the pasta to a shallow flameproof dish and sprinkle with the grated cheese.

5 Cook under a preheated hot broiler for 5 minutes, until the cheese is golden brown and bubbling. Transfer to 4 serving plates and garnish with basil sprigs. Serve immediately.

tagliatelle & garlic sauce

serves four

2 tbsp walnut oil

1 bunch scallions, sliced

2 garlic cloves, sliced thinly

8 oz/225 g mushrooms, sliced

1 lb 2 oz/500 g fresh green and
white tagliatelle

1 cup frozen chopped leaf spinach,
thawed and drained

½ cup full-fat soft cheese flavored
with garlic and herbs

4 tbsp light cream

½ cup chopped, unsalted
pistachio nuts

2 tbsp shredded fresh basil

salt and pepper

4 fresh basil sprigs, to garnish

Italian bread, to serve

1 Heat the walnut oil in a skillet over a low heat. Add the scallions and garlic and cook for 1 minute, or until just softened. Add the mushrooms, stir well, cover, and cook gently for about 5 minutes, or until softened.

2 Meanwhile, bring a large pan of lightly salted water to a boil over a medium heat. Add the pasta and cook for 3–5 minutes, or until just done. Drain the pasta thoroughly and return to the pan.

3 Add the spinach to the mushrooms and heat through for 1–2 minutes. Add the cheese and let melt slightly. Stir in the cream and heat without letting it boil.

4 Pour the vegetable mixture over the pasta, season to taste with salt and pepper, and mix well. Heat gently, stirring, for 2–3 minutes.

5 Transfer the pasta to a large, warmed serving plates and sprinkle over the pistachio nuts and shredded basil. Garnish with fresh basil sprigs and serve with Italian bread.

spicy tomato tagliatelle

serves four

3 tbsp butter

1 onion, chopped finely

1 garlic clove, minced

2 small fresh red chiles, seeded
   and diced

1 lb/450 g fresh tomatoes, peeled,
   seeded, and diced

¾ cup vegetable bouillon

2 tbsp tomato paste

1 tsp sugar

salt and pepper

1 lb 7 oz/650 g fresh green
   and white tagliatelle, or
   12 oz/350 g dried tagliatelle

VARIATION

Try topping your pasta
dish with 1¾ oz/50 g pancetta or
unsmoked bacon, diced and
dry fried for 5 minutes,
or until crispy.

1 Melt the butter in a large pan over a low heat. Add the onion and garlic and cook for 3–4 minutes, or until softened.

2 Add the chiles to the pan and continue cooking for about 2 minutes.

3 Add the tomatoes and bouillon, then reduce the heat and simmer for 10 minutes, stirring.

4 Pour the sauce into a food processor and blend for 1 minute, or until smooth. Alternatively, rub the sauce through a strainer.

5 Return the sauce to the pan and add the tomato paste, sugar, and salt and pepper to taste. Gently heat over a low heat, until piping hot.

6 Bring a large pan of lightly salted water to a boil over a medium heat. Add the pasta and cook until just done. Drain the pasta and transfer to 4 warmed serving plates, and serve with the tomato sauce.

tagliatelle with pumpkin

serves four

1 lb 2 oz/500 g pumpkin or
   butternut squash
2 tbsp olive oil
1 onion, chopped finely
2 garlic cloves, minced
4–6 tbsp chopped fresh parsley
good pinch of ground or freshly
   grated nutmeg
about 1 cup chicken or
   vegetable bouillon
4½ oz/125 g prosciutto, cut into
   narrow strips
9 oz/275 g dried tagliatelle
⅔ cup heavy cream
salt and pepper
freshly grated Parmesan cheese,
   to serve

1 Peel the pumpkin or squash
and scoop out the seeds and
membrane. Cut the flesh into ½-inch/
1-cm dice.

2 Heat the oil in a pan over a low
heat. Add the onion and garlic
and cook until softened. Add half the
parsley and cook for 1–2 minutes.

3 Add the pumpkin or squash and
cook for 2–3 minutes. Season
well with salt, pepper, and nutmeg.

4 Add half the bouillon, bring to
a boil over a medium heat, cover
and simmer for about 10 minutes, or
until the pumpkin is tender, adding
more bouillon as necessary. Add the
prosciutto and continue to cook for
2 minutes, stirring frequently.

5 Meanwhile, bring a large pan of
lightly salted water to a boil over
a medium heat. Add the pasta and
cook until just done. Drain the pasta
thoroughly and transfer to a large,
warmed serving dish.

6 Add the cream to the ham
mixture and heat. Season to taste
and spoon over the pasta. Sprinkle
with the remaining parsley and serve
with the Parmesan cheese.

fettuccine all'alfredo

1 Put the butter and ⅝ cup of the cream in a large pan and bring the mixture to a boil over a medium heat. Reduce the heat, then simmer gently for about 1½ minutes, or until thickened slightly.

2 Meanwhile, bring a large pan of lightly salted water to a boil over a medium heat. Add the pasta and oil and cook for 2–3 minutes, or until just done. Drain the pasta thoroughly, then pour over the cream sauce.

3 Toss the pasta in the sauce over a low heat until coated thoroughly.

4 Add the remaining cream, the Parmesan cheese, and nutmeg to the pasta mixture and season to taste with salt and pepper. Toss thoroughly while gently heating through.

5 Transfer the pasta mixture to a large, warmed serving plate and garnish with a fresh parsley sprig. Serve immediately, with extra Parmesan cheese if you wish.

fettuccine & walnut sauce

serves four to six

2 thick slices whole-wheat bread,
  crusts removed

1¼ cups milk

2½ cups shelled walnuts

2 garlic cloves, minced

1 cup pitted ripe black olives

⅔ cup freshly grated
  Parmesan cheese

8 tbsp extra virgin olive oil

⅝ cup heavy cream

1 lb/450 g fresh fettuccine

2–3 tbsp chopped fresh parsley

salt and pepper

1 Put the bread into a large shallow dish. Pour over the milk and set aside to soak until all the liquid has been absorbed.

2 Spread the walnuts out onto a large cookie sheet and toast in a preheated oven at 375°F/190°C, for about 5 minutes, or until golden. Let cool.

3 Put the soaked bread, walnuts, garlic, olives, Parmesan cheese, and 6 tablespoons of the oil into a food processor and process to make a paste. Season to taste with salt and pepper, then stir in the cream.

4 Bring a large pan of lightly salted water to a boil over a medium heat. Add the pasta and 1 teaspoon of the remaining oil, and cook for about 2–3 minutes, or until just done. Drain the pasta thoroughly and toss with the remaining oil.

5 Transfer the pasta to large serving plates and spoon the olive, garlic, and walnut sauce on top. Sprinkle over the parsley and serve immediately.

pasta & chili tomatoes

serves four

10 oz/280 g dried pappardelle

3 tbsp groundnut oil

2 garlic cloves, minced

2 shallots, sliced

8 oz/225 g green beans, sliced

3½ oz/100 g cherry tomatoes, halved

1 tsp chili flakes

4 tbsp crunchy peanut butter

⅔ cup coconut milk

1 tbsp tomato paste

VARIATION

Add slices of chicken or beef to the recipe and stir-fry with the beans and pasta in step 3 for a more substantial main meal.

1 Bring a large pan of lightly salted water to a boil over a medium heat. Add the pasta and cook for about 8–10 minutes, or until just done. Drain thoroughly and set aside.

2 Meanwhile, heat a large wok over a medium heat. Add the oil and when hot, add the garlic and shallots. Cook for 1 minute.

3 Add the green beans and drained pasta to the wok and cook, stirring, for 5 minutes. Add the cherry tomatoes and mix well.

4 Mix the chili flakes, peanut butter, coconut milk, and tomato paste. Pour the chili mixture into the wok, toss well and heat through.

5 Transfer the pasta to 4 large, warmed serving dishes and serve immediately.

chile & bell pepper pasta

serves four

2 red bell peppers, halved
and seeded

1 small fresh red chile

4 tomatoes, halved

2 garlic cloves

½ cup ground almonds

7 tbsp olive oil

1 lb 7 oz/650 g fresh pasta or
12 oz/350 g dried pasta

fresh oregano leaves, to garnish

VARIATION

Add 2 tablespoons of red wine
vinegar to the sauce and use as
a dressing for a cold pasta salad,
if you wish.

---

1 Put the peppers, skin-side up, onto a cookie sheet with the chile and tomatoes, skin-side down. Cook under a preheated hot broiler for 15 minutes or until charred. After 10 minutes turn the tomatoes over. Put the peppers and chiles into a plastic bag and set aside for 10 minutes.

2 Peel the skins from the bell peppers and chile and slice the flesh into strips. Peel the garlic, and peel, and seed the tomato halves.

3 Put the ground almonds onto a cookie sheet and put under the broiler for 2–3 minutes until golden.

4 Put the bell peppers, chile, garlic, and tomatoes into a processor and process until smooth. With the motor still running, slowly add the oil through the feeder tube to form a thick sauce. Alternatively, put the mixture into a bowl and mash with a fork. Beat in the oil, drop by drop.

5 Stir the toasted ground almonds into the mixture. Warm the sauce in a pan until it is heated through.

6 Bring a large pan of lightly salted water to a boil over a medium heat. Add the pasta and cook for until just done. Drain the pasta thoroughly and transfer to a large, warmed serving dish. Pour over the sauce and toss to mix. Garnish with fresh oregano leaves and serve.

vegetables & beancurd

serves four

8 oz/225 g asparagus spears

4 oz/115 g snow peas

8 oz/225 g green beans

1 leek

8 oz/225 g shelled small fava beans

2½ cups dried fusilli

2 tbsp olive oil

2 tbsp butter

1 garlic clove, minced

8 oz/225 g beancurd, cut into
    1-inch/2.5-cm cubes
    (drained weight)

½ cup pitted green olives in
    brine, drained

salt and pepper

freshly grated Parmesan cheese,
    to serve

1 Cut the asparagus into 2-inch/
5-cm lengths. Thinly slice the
snow peas diagonally and slice the
green beans into 1-inch/2.5-cm pieces.
Thinly slice the leek.

2 Bring a large pan of water to a
boil over a medium heat. Add the
asparagus, green beans, and fava
beans. Bring back to a boil and cook
for 4 minutes. Drain well, rinse in cold
water, and drain again. Set aside.

3 Bring a large pan of lightly salted
water to a boil over a medium
heat. Add the pasta and cook for
8–10 minutes, or until done. Drain
and toss in 1 tablespoon of the oil.
Season to taste with salt and pepper.

4 Meanwhile, heat the remaining
oil and the butter in a wok and
add the leek, garlic, and beancurd.
Cook gently for 1–2 minutes, or until
the vegetables have just softened.

5 Stir in the snow peas and cook for
1 additional minute.

6 Add the blanched vegetables and
olives to the wok and heat
through for 1 minute. Carefully stir in
the pasta and adjust the seasoning, if
necessary. Cook for 1 minute and pile
into a warmed serving dish. Serve
sprinkled with Parmesan cheese.

pasta with nuts & cheese

serves four

1 cup pine nuts

3 cups dried pasta shapes

2 zucchini, sliced

1¼ cups broccoli flowerets

1 cup full-fat soft cheese

⅔ cup milk

1 tbsp chopped fresh basil

4½ oz/125 g white
    mushrooms, sliced

3 oz/85 g blue cheese, crumbled

salt and pepper

1 fresh basil sprig, to garnish

salad greens, to serve

1 Sprinkle the pine nuts on a cookie sheet. Put under a preheated hot broiler and cook, turning occasionally, until lightly browned. Set aside.

2 bring a large pan of lightly salted water to a boil over a medium heat. Add the pasta and cook for 8–10 minutes, or until just done.

3 Meanwhile, cook the zucchini and broccoli in a small amount of boiling, lightly salted water for about 5 minutes, or until just tender.

4 Put the soft cheese into a pan and heat gently, stirring. Add the milk and stir to mix. Add the basil and mushrooms and cook for 2–3 minutes. Stir in the blue cheese and season to taste with salt and pepper.

5 Drain the pasta and vegetables and mix together Pour over the sauce and add the pine nuts. Toss gently and garnish with a basil sprig. Serve with salad greens.

italian tomato sauce & pasta

serves two

1 tbsp olive oil

1 small onion, chopped finely

1–2 cloves garlic, minced

12 oz/350 g tomatoes, peeled
   and chopped

2 tsp tomato paste

2 tbsp water

2¾–3 cups dried pasta shapes

¾ cup lean bacon, derinded
   and diced

½ cup mushrooms, sliced

1 tbsp chopped fresh parsley or
   1 tsp chopped fresh cilantro

2 tbsp sour cream, optional

salt and pepper

COOK'S TIP

Sour cream contains
18–20% fat, so if you are
following a lowfat diet you can
leave it out of this recipe or
substitute a lowfat alternative.

1 Heat the oil in a pan over a low
heat. Add the onion and garlic,
and cook gently until soft.

2 Add the tomatoes, tomato paste,
and water. Season to taste with
salt and pepper and bring to a boil
over a low heat. Cover and simmer
gently for 10 minutes.

3 Bring a large pan of lightly salted
water to a boil over a medium
heat. Add the pasta and cook until just
done. Drain thoroughly and transfer to
2 warmed serving dishes.

4 Heat the bacon gently in a skillet
over a low heat until the fat runs,
then add the mushrooms and cook for
3–4 minutes. Drain off any excess oil.

5 Add the bacon and mushrooms to
the tomato mixture, together with
the parsley or cilantro and the sour
cream. Heat through gently and serve
immediately with the pasta.

macaroni & corn crêpes

serves four

2 corn cobs

4 tbsp butter

115 g/4 oz red bell peppers, seeded
 and diced finely

1¼ cups dried short-cut macaroni

½ cup heavy cream

2 tbsp all-purpose flour

4 egg yolks

4 tbsp olive oil

salt and pepper

TO SERVE

oyster mushrooms

cooked leeks

1 Bring a pan of water to a boil over a medium heat. Add the corn cobs and cook for 8 minutes. Drain thoroughly and refresh under cold running water for 3 minutes. Carefully cut away the kernels onto paper towels and let dry.

2 Melt 2 tablespoons of the butter in a large skillet over a low heat. Add the bell peppers and cook for about 4 minutes. Drain and pat dry on paper towels.

3 Bring a large pan of lightly salted water to a boil over a medium heat. Add the macaroni and cook for about 12 minutes, or until done. Drain the macaroni thoroughly and let cool in cold water until required.

4 Beat the cream with the flour, a pinch of salt, and the egg yolks in a bowl until smooth. Add the corn and bell peppers. Drain the macaroni, then toss into the corn and cream mixture. Season with pepper to taste.

5 Heat the remaining butter with the oil in a skillet. Drop spoonfuls of the mixture into the skillet and press down to form flat crêpes. Cook until golden, and all the mixture is used up. Serve with mushrooms and leeks.

three-cheese macaroni

serves four

2 cups Bechamel sauce

2 cups dried macaroni

1 egg, beaten

1¼ cups freshly grated sharp
   cheddar cheese

1 tbsp whole-grain mustard

2 tbsp chopped fresh chives

4 tomatoes, sliced

1¼ cups freshly grated brick cheese

½ cup freshly grated blue cheese

2 tbsp sunflower seeds

salt and pepper

snipped fresh chives, to garnish

1 Make the Bechamel sauce, transfer it into a bowl, and cover with plastic wrap to prevent a skin forming on the surface of the sauce. Set aside.

2 Bring a pan of lightly salted water to a boil over a medium heat. Add the macaroni and cook for 8–10 minutes. or until just done. Drain and put into a greased ovenproof dish.

3 Stir the beaten egg, cheddar cheese, mustard, and chives into the Bechamel sauce and season to taste with salt and pepper.

4 Spoon the sauce over the macaroni, making sure it is well covered. Arrange the sliced tomatoes in a layer over the top.

5 Sprinkle the brick and blue cheeses and the sunflower seeds evenly over the pasta bake. Put the dish on a cookie sheet and cook in a preheated oven at 190°C/375°F, for 25–30 minutes, or until the topping is bubbling and golden.

6 Garnish the pasta bake with snipped chives and serve immediately on 4 warmed plates.

spaghetti & salmon sauce

serves four

1 lb 2 oz/500 g dried
buckwheat spaghetti

1 tbsp olive oil

½ cup feta cheese, crumbled
(drained weight)

1 tbsp fresh cilantro or parsley,
to garnish

SAUCE

1¼ cups heavy cream

⅔ cup whiskey or brandy

4½ oz/125 g smoked salmon

large pinch of cayenne pepper

2 tbsp chopped fresh cilantro
or parsley

salt and pepper

1 Bring a large pan of lightly salted water to a boil over a medium heat. Add the pasta and 1 teaspoon of the oil, and cook for 8–10 minutes, or until done. Drain the pasta thoroughly, then return the pasta to the pan, sprinkle over the remaining oil, cover and shake well. Set aside and keep warm until required.

2 To make the sauce, heat the cream and whiskey or brandy in separate small pans, to simmering point. Do not let them boil.

3 Mix the cream with the whiskey or brandy together in a bowl.

4 Cut the smoked salmon into thin strips and add to the cream mixture. Season to taste with a little pepper and cayenne pepper, then stir in the chopped cilantro or parsley.

5 Transfer the pasta to a large, warmed serving dish, pour on the sauce and toss thoroughly with 2 large forks. Sprinkle the crumbled cheese over the pasta and garnish with the chopped cilantro or parsley. Serve immediately.

vermicelli & clam sauce

serves four

14 oz/400 g dried vermicelli,
    spaghetti or other long pasta

1 tbsp olive oil

2 tbsp butter

2 onions, chopped

2 garlic cloves, chopped

400 g/14 oz bottled clams in brine

½ cup white wine

4 tbsp chopped fresh parsley

½ tsp dried oregano

pinch of freshly grated nutmeg

salt and pepper

2 tbsp fresh Parmesan
    cheese shavings

1 fresh basil sprig, to garnish

1 Bring a large pan of lightly salted water to a boil over a medium heat. Add the pasta and and cook until just done. Drain, then return to the pan and add the butter. Cover the pan and shake well. Keep warm.

2 Heat the oil in a pan over a medium heat. Add the onions and cook until translucent. Stir in the garlic and cook for 1 minute.

3 Strain the liquid from the bottled clams into bowl. Add half of it to the pan with the white wine and discard the remaining liquid. Stir, then bring to simmering point and simmer for 3 minutes.

4 Add the clams, parsley, and oregano to the pan and season to taste with pepper and nutmeg. Reduce the heat and cook until the sauce is heated through.

5 Transfer the pasta to a warmed serving dish and pour over the sauce. Sprinkle with the Parmesan cheese, garnish with the basil and serve immediately.

pasta & mussel sauce

serves six

3½ cups pasta shells

1 tsp olive oil

SAUCE

6 pints/3.5 litres mussels, scrubbed

1 cup dry white wine

2 large onions, chopped

½ cup sweet butter

6 large garlic cloves, chopped finely

5 tbsp chopped fresh parsley

1¼ cups heavy cream

salt and pepper

1 To make the sauce, pull off the "beards" from the mussels and rinse well in several changes of water. Discard any mussels that refuse to close when tapped. Put the mussels into a large pan with the wine and half the onions. Cover, shake and cook over a medium heat for about 2–3 minutes, or until the mussels open.

2 Remove the pan from the heat, lift out the mussels with a slotted spoon and set aside the liquid. Let cool. Discard any mussels that have not opened.

3 Melt the butter in a pan over a medium heat. Add the remaining onion and cook for 3–4 minutes, or until translucent. Stir in the garlic and cook for 1 minute. Gradually pour on the reserved cooking liquid, stirring to blend thoroughly. Stir in the parsley and cream. Season to taste with salt and pepper and bring to simmering point. Taste and adjust the seasoning, if necessary.

4 Bring a pan of lightly salted water to a boil over a medium heat. Add the pasta and oil and cook until done. Drain and return to the pan.

5 Remove the mussels from their shells and set aside a few shells. Stir the mussels into the cream sauce. Tip the pasta into a dish, pour on the sauce and mix. Garnish with a few of the reserved mussel shells and serve.

pasta vongole

serves four

1 lb 7 oz/650 g fresh clams or
   10 oz280 g canned
   clams, drained

2 tbsp olive oil

2 cloves garlic, chopped finely

14 oz/400 g mixed seafood, such
   as shrimp, squid, and mussels,
   thawed if frozen

⅔ cup white wine

⅔ cup fish bouillon

2 tbsp chopped tarragon

salt and pepper

1 lb 7 oz/650 g fresh pasta or
   12 oz/350 g dried pasta

VARIATION

Red clam sauce can be made by
adding 8 tbsp of tomato paste to
the sauce along with the bouillon
in step 4. Follow
the same cooking method.

---

1 If you are using fresh clams, scrub them clean and discard any that are already open.

2 Heat the oil in a large skillet over a medium heat. Add the garlic and the clams and cook for 2 minutes, shaking the pan to ensure that all of the clams are coated in the oil.

3 Add the remaining seafood mixture to the skillet and cook for an additional 2 minutes.

4 Pour the wine and bouillon over the mixed seafood and garlic. Bring to a boil over a medium heat. Cover, then reduce the heat and simmer for 8–10 minutes, or until the shells open. Discard any clams or mussels that refuse to open.

5 Bring a large pan of lightly salted water to a boil over a medium heat. Add the pasta and cook until just done. Drain thoroughly.

6 Stir the chopped tarragon into the sauce and season to taste with salt and pepper.

7 Transfer the pasta to a plate and pour over the sauce. Serve.

macaroni & squid casserole

serves six

2 cups dried short-cut macaroni, or
  other short pasta shapes

1 tsp olive oil

2 tbsp chopped fresh parsley

salt and pepper

SAUCE

12 oz/350 g cleaned squid, cut into
  ½-inch/4-cm strips

6 tbsp olive oil

2 onions, sliced

1 cup fish bouillon

⅔ cup red wine

12 oz/350 g tomatoes, peeled and
  sliced thinly

2 tbsp tomato paste

1 tsp dried oregano

2 bay leaves

1. Bring a large pan of lightly salted water to a boil over a medium heat. Add the pasta and oil, and cook for 3 minutes. Drain well, return to the pan, cover and keep warm.

2. To make the sauce, heat the oil in a skillet over a medium heat. Add the onion and cook until translucent. Add the squid and bouillon and cook for 5 minutes. Pour over the wine and add the tomatoes, tomato paste, oregano, and bay leaves. Bring to a boil, season to taste with salt and pepper, and cook for 5 minutes.

3. Add the pasta, stir well, cover, and simmer for 10 minutes, or until the macaroni and squid are almost tender. By this time the sauce should be thick and syrupy. If it is too liquid, uncover the pan and continue cooking for a few minutes. Taste and adjust the seasoning. if necessary.

4. Remove the bay leaves and stir in most of the chopped parsley, and set aside a little to garnish. Transfer to a warmed serving dish. Sprinkle on the remaining parsley and serve.

pasta with sicilian sauce

serves four

1 lb/450 g tomatoes, halved

¼ cup pine nuts

⅓ cup golden raisins

1¾ oz/50 g canned anchovy fillets,
  drained and halved lengthwise

2 tbsp concentrated tomato paste

1 lb 7 oz/650 g fresh penne or
  12 oz/350 g dried penne

COOK'S TIP

If you are making fresh pasta,
remember that pasta dough
prefers warm conditions and
responds well to handling. Do
not let chill and do not use a
marble counter for kneading.

1 Cook the tomatoes under a
preheated broiler for about
10 minutes. Let cool. Once cool
enough to handle, peel off the skin and
dice the flesh.

2 Place the pine nuts on a cookie
sheet and lightly toast under the
broiler for 2–3 minutes, or until
golden.

3 Soak the golden raisins in a bowl
of warm water for 20 minutes.
Drain the golden raisins thoroughly.

4 Put the tomatoes, pine nuts, and
golden raisins in a pan and heat.

5 Add the anchovies and tomato
paste and cook until hot.

6 Bring a large pan of lightly salted
water to a boil over a medium
heat. Add the pasta and cook until
done. Drain thoroughly.

7 Transfer the pasta to a large
serving plate and serve with the
hot Sicilian sauce.

milanese risotto

serves four

2 good pinches of saffron threads

6 tbsp butter

1 large onion, chopped finely

1–2 garlic cloves, minced

3 cups risotto rice

⅔ cup dry white wine

5 cups boiling vegetable bouillon

¾ cup freshly grated
   Parmesan cheese

salt and pepper

1 Put the saffron into a small bowl, cover with 3–4 tablespoons of boiling water, and let soak while you prepare the risotto.

2 Melt 4 tablespoons of the butter in a pan over a low heat. Add the onion and garlic and cook until soft but not colored. Add the rice and cook for 2–3 minutes, or until the grains are coated in butter and starting to color.

3 Add the wine to the rice and simmer gently, stirring from time to time, until it is all absorbed.

4 Add the boiling bouillon a little at a time, about ⅝ cup, cooking until the liquid is fully absorbed before adding more, and stirring frequently.

5 When all the bouillon has been absorbed (this should take about 20 minutes), the rice should be tender but not soft and soggy. Add the saffron liquid, Parmesan cheese, and remaining butter. Season to taste with salt and pepper. Simmer for 2 minutes until piping hot and thoroughly mixed.

6 Cover the pan tightly and let stand for 5 minutes off the heat. Give a good stir and serve.

sun-dried risotto

about 12 sun-dried tomatoes, not
in oil

2 tbsp olive oil

1 large onion, chopped finely

4–6 garlic cloves, chopped finely

2 cups risotto rice

6¼ cups chicken or vegetable
bouillon, simmering

1 cup frozen peas, thawed

2 tbsp chopped fresh Italian parsley

1 cup freshly grated aged
romano cheese

1 tbsp extra virgin olive oil

1 Put the sun-dried tomatoes into a bowl and pour over enough boiling water to cover. Let stand for about 30 minutes, or until the tomatoes are soft and supple. Drain and dry on paper towels, then shred thinly and set aside.

2 Heat the oil in a large pan over a medium heat. Add the onion and cook for 2 minutes. Add the garlic and cook for 15 seconds, then add the rice and cook for 2 minutes, or until the rice is translucent and coated with oil.

3 Add a ladleful of the hot bouillon: it will bubble and steam rapidly. Cook, stirring continuously, until all the liquid has been absorbed.

4 Continue stirring in the bouillon, about half a ladleful at a time, letting each addition be absorbed by the rice before adding the next.

5 After 15 minutes, stir in the sun-dried tomatoes. Cook, adding the bouillon, until the rice is tender, but firm to the bite. Add the peas with the last addition of the bouillon.

6 Remove from the heat and stir in the parsley and half the cheese. Cover, let stand for 1 minute, then spoon into serving dishes. Drizzle with the oil and sprinkle the remaining cheese over the top. Serve.

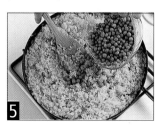

green risotto

serves four

1 onion, chopped

2 tbsp olive oil

1¼ cups risotto rice

1⅓ cups hot vegetable bouillon

12 oz/350 g mixed green vegetables,
   such as asparagus, thin green
   beans, snow peas, zucchini,
   broccoli flowerets, frozen peas

2 tbsp chopped fresh parsley

½ cup fresh Parmesan cheese,
   shaved thinly

salt and pepper

COOK'S TIP

For extra texture, stir in a few
toasted pine nuts or coarsely
chopped cashew nuts at the end
of the cooking time.

1 Put the onion and oil into a large
bowl. Cover and cook in the
microwave on HIGH for 2 minutes.

2 Add the rice and stir until coated
in the oil. Pour in ⅓ cup of the
bouillon. Cook for 2 minutes, until the
liquid has been absorbed. Pour in
another ⅓ cup of the bouillon and cook
on HIGH for 2 minutes. Repeat.

3 Chop the vegetables into even-
size pieces. Stir into the rice with
the remaining bouillon. Cover and cook
on HIGH for 8 minutes, stirring, until
most of the liquid has been absorbed
and the rice is tender.

4 Stir in the chopped parsley and
season generously to taste with
salt and pepper.

5 Let the risotto stand, covered, for
about 5 minutes. The rice should
be tender and creamy.

6 Transfer to a large serving dish
and sprinkle the Parmesan cheese
over the risotto before serving.

exotic mushroom risotto

serves six

¼ cup dried porcini or
  morel mushrooms
about 1 lb 2 oz/500 g mixed fresh
  exotic mushrooms, such as
  porcini, girolles, horse
  mushrooms, and chanterelles,
  halved if large
4 tbsp olive oil
3–4 garlic cloves, chopped finely
4 tbsp sweet butter
1 onion, chopped finely
3 cups risotto rice
¼ cup dry white vermouth
5 cups chicken bouillon, simmering
1⅓ cups freshly grated
  Parmesan cheese
4 tbsp chopped fresh Italian parsley
salt and pepper
6 fresh parsley sprigs, to garnish
crusty bread, to serve

1 Put the dried mushrooms into a bowl and add enough boiling water to cover. Let soak for 30 minutes, then carefully lift out and pat dry. Strain the soaking liquid through a strainer lined with paper towels and set aside.

2 Trim the exotic mushrooms and gently brush clean.

3 Heat 3 tablespoons of the oil in a large skillet over a low heat. Add the mixed fresh mushrooms and cook, stirring, for 1–2 minutes. Add the garlic and the soaked mushrooms, and cook, stirring frequently, for 2 minutes. Transfer to a plate.

4 Heat the remaining oil and half the butter in a large pan over a low heat. Add the onion and cook, stirring occasionally, for 2 minutes until softened. Add the rice and cook, stirring frequently, for about 2 minutes until translucent and well coated.

5 Add the vermouth. When almost absorbed, add a ladleful (about 1 cup) of the bouillon. Cook, stirring continuously, until the liquid is absorbed.

6 Continue adding the bouillon, about half a ladleful at a time, letting each addition to be completely absorbed before adding the next. This should take 20–25 minutes. The risotto should have a creamy consistency and the rice should be tender, but firm to the bite.

7 Add half the reserved mushroom soaking liquid to the risotto and stir in the mushrooms. Season to taste with salt and pepper and add more mushroom liquid, if necessary. Remove the pan from the heat and stir in the remaining butter, the Parmesan cheese, and parsley. Transfer the risotto to 6 warmed dishes, garnish with parsley sprigs and serve immediately.

rice & peas

serves four

1 tbsp olive oil

4 tbsp butter

2oz/55 g pancetta or lean
   bacon, chopped

1 small onion, chopped

6 cups hot chicken bouillon

1¾ cups risotto rice

3 tbsp chopped fresh parsley

2 cups frozen or canned baby peas

½ cup freshly grated Parmesan
   cheese

pepper

1 Heat the oil and half the butter in a large pan over a low heat. Add the pancetta or bacon and onion and cook, stirring occasionally, for about 5 minutes, or until the onion is translucent, but not browned.

2 Add the bouillon to the pan and bring to a boil over a medium heat. Stir in the rice and season to taste with pepper. Bring to a boil, reduce the heat, and simmer, stirring occasionally, for about 20–30 minutes, or until the rice is tender, but still firm to the bite.

3 Add the parsley and frozen or canned baby peas and cook for about 8 minutes, or until the peas are heated through. Stir in the remaining butter and the Parmesan cheese.

4 Transfer the risottos to a large warmed serving dish and serve immediately with pepper.

pesto rice with garlic bread

serves four

2¾ oz mixed long-grain and
    wild rice
fresh basil sprigs, to garnish
tomato and orange salad, to serve
PESTO SAUCE
4 tbsp fresh basil sprigs
1¼ cups pine nuts
2 garlic cloves, minced
6 tbsp olive oil
½ cup freshly grated
    Parmesan cheese
GARLIC BREAD
2 small granary or whole-wheat
    French bread sticks
5 tbsp butter , softened
2 garlic cloves, minced
1 tsp dried mixed herbs
salt and pepper

1 Put the rice in a pan and cover with water. Bring to a boil over a medium heat and cook for about 15–20 minutes. Drain and keep warm.

2 To make the pesto sauce, remove the basil leaves from the stalks and finely chop the leaves. Set aside ¼ cup of the pine nuts and finely chop the remainder. Mix with the chopped basil and the rest of the dressing ingredients. Alternatively, put all the ingredients into a food processor or blender and process for a few seconds until smooth. Set aside.

3 To make the garlic bread, slice the bread at 1 inch/2.5 cm intervals, taking care not to slice all the way through. Mix the butter with the garlic, and herbs. Season to taste with salt and pepper. Spread thickly between each slice.

4 Wrap the bread in foil and cook in a preheated oven at 200°C/400°F, for 10–15 minutes.

5 To serve, toast the reserved pine nuts under a preheated medium-hot broiler for 2–3 minutes, or until golden. Toss the pesto sauce into the hot rice and pile into a warmed serving dish. Sprinkle with toasted pine nuts and garnish with a few basil sprigs. Serve with the garlic bread and a tomato and orange salad.

green easter pie

1 tbsp butter for greasing

3 oz/85 g arugula

2 tbsp olive oil

1 onion, chopped

2 garlic cloves, chopped

1 cup risotto rice

3 cups hot chicken or
   vegetable bouillon

½ cup white wine

⅔ cup freshly grated
   Parmesan cheese

1 cup frozen peas, thawed

2 tomatoes, diced

4 eggs, beaten

3 tbsp chopped fresh marjoram

1 cup fresh bread crumbs

salt and pepper

1 Grease a 9-inch/23-cm deep cake pan and line the bottom.

2 Using a sharp knife, coarsely chop the arugula.

3 Heat the oil in a skillet over a low heat. Add the onion and garlic and cook for 4–5 minutes.

4 Add the rice to the skillet, mix well, then start adding the bouillon a ladleful at a time. Wait until each ladleful of bouillon has been absorbed before adding the next.

5 Continue to cook the mixture, adding the wine, until the rice is tender. This will take at least 15 minutes. Remove the skillet from the heat.

6 Stir in the Parmesan cheese, peas, arugula, tomatoes, eggs, and 2 tablespoons of the marjoram. Season to taste with salt and pepper.

7 Spoon the risotto into the prepared pan and level the surface by pressing down with the back of a wooden spoon.

8 Top with the bread crumbs and the remaining marjoram.

9 Cook in a preheated oven at 350°F/180°C, for 30 minutes, or until set. Cut into slices and serve.

genoese seafood risotto

serves four

5 cups hot fish or chicken bouillon

3 cups risotto rice

3 tbsp butter

2 garlic cloves, chopped

9 oz/250 g mixed seafood,
preferably raw, such as shrimp,
squid, mussels, and clams

2 tbsp chopped oregano, plus extra
for garnishing

½ cup freshly grated romano or
Parmesan cheese

COOK'S TIP

The Genoese are excellent cooks,
and they make particularly
delicious fish dishes, which are
delicately flavored with the
local olive oil.

1 In a large pan, bring the bouillon to a boil over a medium heat. Add the rice and cook for 12 minutes, stirring, until the rice is tender. Drain and set aside any excess liquid.

2 Heat the butter in a large skillet and add the garlic, stirring.

3 Add the seafood to the skillet and cook for 5 minutes. If the seafood is cooked, cook for about 2–3 minutes.

4 Stir the oregano into the seafood mixture in the skillet.

5 Add the rice to the skillet and cook for 2–3 minutes, stirring, until hot. Add the reserved bouillon if the mixture gets too sticky. Add the romano or Parmesan cheese and mix.

6 Transfer the risotto to 4 large, warmed serving dishes and serve.

chicken risotto milanese

serves four–six

½–1 tsp saffron threads

5⅔ cups chicken
   bouillon, simmering

6 tbsp unsalted butter

2–3 shallots, chopped finely

2 cups risotto rice

2 cups freshly grated
   Parmesan cheese

salt and pepper

1 Put the saffron threads into a small bowl. Pour over enough of the bouillon to cover the threads, then set aside to infuse.

2 Melt 2 tablespoons of the butter in a large pan over a medium heat. Add the shallots and cook for about 2 minutes, or until starting to soften. Add the rice and cook, stirring frequently, for about 2 minutes, or until the rice is starting to turn translucent and is coated with the butter.

3 Add a ladleful (about 1 cup) of the bouillon; it will steam and bubble. Cook, stirring continuously, until the liquid is absorbed.

4 Continue adding the bouillon, about half a ladleful at a time, allowing each addition to be absorbed before adding the next. Don't let the rice cook "dry."

5 After about 15 minutes, stir in the saffron-infused bouillon; the rice will turn a vibrant yellow and the color will become deeper as it cooks. Continue cooking, adding the bouillon in the same way until the rice is tender, but still firm to the bite. The risotto should have a creamy consistency.

6 Stir in the remaining butter and half the Parmesan cheese, then remove from the heat. Cover and let stand for about 1 minute.

7 Spoon the risotto into serving bowls and serve immediately with the remaining Parmesan cheese.

spinach & ricotta gnocchi

serves four

2 lb 4 oz/1 kg spinach

2 cups ricotta cheese

1¼ cups freshly grated
    romano cheese

3 eggs, beaten

¼ tsp freshly grated nutmeg

all-purpose flour, to mix

dash of olive oil

9 tbsp sweet butter

¼ cup pine nuts

⅓ cup raisins

salt and pepper

1 Wash and drain the spinach. Cook in a covered pan without any extra liquid until soft, 8 minutes. Put the spinach into a strainer and press well to remove as much liquid as possible. Put the spinach into a blender and process until smooth. Alternatively, rub the spinach through a strainer.

2 Mix the spinach puree with the ricotta cheese, half the romano cheese, the eggs, and nutmeg. Season to taste with salt and pepper, mixing lightly but thoroughly. Work in enough flour, lightly and quickly, to make the mixture easy to handle.

3 Shape the dough quickly into small lozenge shapes, and dust lightly with a little flour.

4 Add a dash of oil to a large pan of salted water and bring to a boil over a medium heat. Add the gnocchi carefully and boil for about 2 minutes, or until they float to the surface. Using a slotted spoon, transfer the gnocchi to a buttered ovenproof dish. Keep warm.

5 Melt the butter in a small skillet over a low heat. Add the pine nuts and raisins and cook until the nuts start to brown slightly, but do not let the butter burn.

6 Transfer the gnocchi to 4 dishes, pour the mixture over and add the remaining cheese. Serve.

potato & spinach gnocchi

serves four

1⅔ cups diced mealy potatoes

6 oz/175 g spinach

1 egg yolk

1 tsp olive oil

1 cup all-purpose flour

salt and pepper

fresh spinach leaves, to garnish

SAUCE

1 tbsp olive oil

2 shallots, chopped

1 garlic clove, minced

1¼ cups strained tomatoes

2 tsp soft light brown sugar

1 Bring a pan of water to a boil over a medium heat. Add the potatoes and cook for 10 minutes, then drain and mash.

2 Blanch the spinach in a little boiling water for 1–2 minutes. Drain and shred the leaves.

3 Transfer the mashed potato to a lightly floured cutting board and make a well in the center. Add the egg yolk, oil, spinach, and a little of the flour. Quickly mix the ingredients into the potato, adding more flour, until you have a firm dough. Divide the mixture into very small dumplings.

4 Bring a large pan of lightly salted water to a boil over a medium heat, Add the gnocchi, in batches, and cook for about 5 minutes, or until they rise to the surface.

5 To make the sauce. Put the oil, shallots, garlic, strained tomatoes, and sugar into a pan and cook over a low heat for 10–15 minutes. or until the sauce has thickened.

6 Drain the gnocchi with a slotted spoon and transfer to 4 warmed serving dishes. Spoon the sauce over the gnocchi and garnish with the fresh spinach leaves. Serve.

baked semolina gnocchi

serves four

2 cups vegetable bouillon

⅔ cup semolina

1 tbsp fresh thyme, stalks removed

1 egg, beaten

½ cup freshly grated
   Parmesan cheese

3 tbsp butter

2 garlic cloves, minced

salt and pepper

1 Put the bouillon into a large pan and bring to a boil over a medium heat. Add the semolina in a steady trickle, stirring continuously. Keep stirring for 3–4 minutes until the mixture is thick enough to hold a spoon upright. Let cool slightly.

2 Add the thyme leaves, egg, and half the cheese to the semolina mixture, and season to taste with salt and pepper.

3 Spread the semolina mixture onto a board to a thickness of about ½ inch/12 mm, and let stand until it has cooled and set.

4 When the semolina is cold, cut it into 1-inch.2.5-cm squares, and set aside any offcuts.

5 Grease an ovenproof dish, putting the reserved offcuts in the bottom. Arrange the semolina squares on top and sprinkle with the remaining cheese.

6 Melt the butter in a pan over a low heat. Add the garlic and season with pepper to taste. Pour the butter mixture over the gnocchi. Cook in a preheated oven at 220°C/425°F, for 15–20 minutes, or until the gnocchi are puffed up and golden. Serve.

polenta kabobs

serves four

1 cup instant polenta

scant 3¾ cups water

2 tbsp fresh thyme, stalks removed

8 slices prosciutto (about 2¾ oz)

1 tbsp olive oil

salt and pepper

salad greens, to serve

COOK'S TIP

Try flavoring the polenta
with chopped oregano, basil,
or marjoram instead of the
thyme, if you prefer. You
should use 1½ tbsp of chopped
fresh herbs to every 1 cup
instant polenta.

---

1 Cook the polenta with the water, stirring occasionally. Alternatively, follow the package instructions.

2 Add the fresh thyme leaves to the polenta mixture and season to taste with salt and pepper.

3 Spread out the polenta, about 1-inch/2.5-cm thick, onto a cutting board. Let cool.

4 Using a sharp knife, cut the cooled polenta into 1-inch/2.5-cm cubes.

5 Cut the prosciutto slices into 2 pieces lengthwise. Wrap the prosciutto around the polenta cubes.

6 Thread the polenta cubes onto presoaked wooden skewers.

7 Brush the kabobs with oil and cook under a preheated hot broiler, turning, for 7–8 minutes. Alternatively, grill the kabobs until golden. Transfer to 4 serving plates and serve with salad greens.

Desserts

For many people the favorite part of any meal

is the desserts. The recipes that have been

selected here will be a treat for all palates.

Whether you are a chocolate-lover or are even on a diet, in this chapter there

is a recipe to tempt you. Choose from a light summer delicacy or a hearty hot

winter treat, you will find plenty of desserts to indulge in all year round. If you

are looking for an afternoon treat, choose the Banana & Lime Cake or Carrot &

Ginger Cake, or if a sumptuous dessert takes your fancy, Chocolate Zabaglione

will definitely do the trick.

carrot & ginger cake

serves ten

1 tbsp butter for greasing

2 cups all-purpose flour

1 tsp baking powder

1 tsp baking soda

2 tsp ground ginger

½ tsp salt

¾ cup molasses sugar

1⅔ cups grated carrots

2 pieces chopped preserved ginger

1 tbsp grated fresh gingerroot

generous ⅓ cup seedless raisins

2 eggs, beaten

3 tbsp corn oil

juice of 1 orange

FROSTING

1 cup lowfat soft cheese

4 tbsp confectioners' sugar

1 tsp vanilla extract

TO DECORATE

grated carrot

finely chopped preserved ginger

ground ginger

1 Grease and line an 8-inch/20-cm round cake pan with a piece of baking parchment.

2 Sift the flour, baking powder, baking soda, ground ginger, and salt into a bowl. Stir in the sugar, carrots, preserved ginger, fresh ginger root, and raisins. Beat the eggs, oil, and orange juice together, then pour into the bowl. Mix all the ingredients together well.

3 Spoon the mixture into the pan and cook in a preheated oven at 350°F/180°C, for 1–1¼ hours, or until a toothpick inserted into the center of the cake comes out clean.

4 To make the frosting, put the soft cheese in a bowl and beat to soften. Sift in the confectioners' sugar and add the vanilla extract. Mix well.

5 Remove the cake from the pan and smooth the frosting over the top. Decorate with the carrot and ginger. Serve.

banana & lime cake

serves ten

1 tbsp butter for greasing

generous 2 cups all-purpose flour

1 tsp salt

1½ tsp baking powder

scant 1 cup light brown sugar

1 tsp lime peel, grated

1 egg, beaten lightly

1 banana, mashed with
 1 tbsp lime juice

⅔ cup lowfat plain yogurt

⅔ cup golden raisins

TOPPING

generous 1 cup confectioners' sugar

1–2 tsp lime juice

½ tsp finely grated lime peel

TO DECORATE

banana chips

finely grated lime peel

1 Grease a deep round 7-inch/18-cm cake pan with butter and line with baking parchment.

2 Sift the flour, salt, and baking powder into a mixing bowl and stir in the sugar and lime peel.

3 Make a well in the center and add the egg, banana, yogurt, and golden raisins. Mix until incorporated.

4 Spoon into the pan and level the surface. Cook in a preheated oven at 350°F/180°C, for 40–45 minutes, or until a toothpick inserted in the center comes out clean. Let cool in the pan for 10 minutes, then turn out onto a rack.

5 To make the topping, sift the confectioners' sugar into a small bowl and mix with the lime juice to form a soft, but not too runny frosting. Stir in the grated lime peel. Drizzle the lime frosting over the cake, letting it run down the sides.

6 Decorate the cooled cake with a few banana chips and lime peel. Let the cake stand for 15 minutes so the frosting sets, then serve.

pear & ginger cake

scant 1 cup sweet butter, softened,
  plus extra for greasing

generous ¾ cup superfine sugar

1¼ cups self-rising flour, strained

1 tbsp ground ginger

3 eggs, beaten lightly

1 lb/450 g dessert pears, peeled,
  cored, and sliced thinly

1 tbsp brown sugar

ice cream or cream, to serve

3 Spoon the cake mixture into the prepared pan and level out the surface with a spoon.

4 Arrange the pear slices over the cake mixture. Sprinkle with the brown sugar and dot the top with the remaining butter.

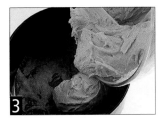

5 Cook in a preheated oven at 350°F/180°C, for 35–40 minutes, or until the cake is golden on top and feels springy to the touch.

6 Serve the pear and ginger cake warm, with ice cream or cream, if you wish.

COOK'S TIP

Store ground ginger in an airtight jar, preferably made of colored glass, or store in a clear glass jar in a cool, dark place.

1 Lightly grease a deep 8-inch/ 20.5-cm cake pan with butter and line with baking parchment.

2 Using a whisk, combine all but 2 tablespoons of the butter with the sugar, flour, ginger, and eggs, and mix to form a smooth consistency.

mascarpone cheesecake

serves eight

4 tbsp sweet butter, plus extra
  for greasing
3 cups ginger cookie crumbs
1 tbsp chopped preserved ginger
2¼ cups mascarpone cheese
finely grated peel and juice of
  2 lemons
½ cup superfine sugar
2 large eggs, separated
fruit coulis (see Cook's Tip), to serve

COOK'S TIP

Fruit coulis can be made by
cooking 14 oz/400 g fruit, such
as blueberries, for 5 minutes
with 2 tbsp of water. Strain the
mixture, then stir in
1 tbsp (or more to taste) of
strained confectioners' sugar. Let
cool before serving.

1 Grease and line the bottom of a 10-inch/25-cm spring-form cake pan or loose-bottomed pan.

2 Melt the butter in a pan over a low heat. Stir in the crushed cookies and ginger. Use the mixture to line the pan, pressing the mixture about ¼ inch/5 mm up the sides.

3 Beat the cheese, lemon peel and juice, sugar, and egg yolks together until quite smooth.

4 Whisk the egg whites in a separate spotlessly clean grease-free until stiff peaks form, then fold into the cheese and lemon mixture.

5 Pour the mixture into the pan and cook in a preheated oven at 350°F/180°C, for 35–45 minutes, or until just set. Don't worry if it cracks or sinks—this is quite normal.

6 Let cool in the pan, then serve the cheesecake with fruit coulis (see Cook's Tip).

tuscan dessert

serves four

1 tbsp butter

⅔ cup mixed dried fruit

generous 1 cup ricotta cheese

3 egg yolks

¼ cup superfine sugar

1 tsp cinnamon

finely grated peel of 1 orange, plus
     extra to decorate

crème fraîche, to serve

COOK'S TIP

Crème fraîche has a slightly sour,
nutty taste and is very thick. It is
suitable for cooking, but has the
same fat content as heavy cream.

1 Grease 4 mini ovenproof bowls or
ramekin dishes with the butter.

2 Put the dried fruit into a bowl and
cover with warm water. Let soak
for 10 minutes.

3 Beat the ricotta cheese with the
egg yolks in a bowl. Stir in the
superfine sugar, cinnamon, and orange
peel and mix.

4 Drain the dried fruit in a strainer
set over a bowl. Mix the drained
fruit with the ricotta cheese mixture.

5 Spoon the mixture into the bowls
or ramekin dishes.

6 Cook in a preheated oven at
350°F/180°C, for 15 minutes. The
tops should just be firm to the touch,
but they should not brown.

7 Decorate the desserts with
some grated orange peel. Serve
warmed or chilled with a spoon of
crème fraîche, if you wish.

summer desserts

serves six

1 tbsp vegetable oil or butter
 for greasing

6–8 thin slices white bread,
 crusts removed

¾ cup superfine sugar

1¼ cups water

1 cup strawberries

2 cups raspberries

¾ cup black and/or red currants

¾ cup blackberries or loganberries

6 fresh mint sprigs, to decorate

pouring cream, to serve

1 Grease 6 ⅔ cup molds with a little butter or oil.

2 Line the molds with the bread, cutting it so it fits snugly.

3 Put the sugar into a pan with the water and heat gently, stirring frequently until dissolved, then bring to a boil over a medium heat and boil for 2 minutes.

4 Set aside 6 large strawberries for decoration. Add half the raspberries and the rest of the fruits to the syrup, cutting the strawberries in half if large, and simmer gently for a few minutes, until they are just soft, but still retain their shape.

5 Spoon the fruits and some of the liquid into the molds. Cover with more bread. Spoon a little juice around the sides of the molds so the bread is well soaked. Cover with a saucer and a heavy weight, let cool, then chill in the refrigerator, preferably overnight.

6 Process the remaining raspberries in a food processor or blender, or press through a non-metallic strainer. Add enough of the liquid from the fruits to give a coating consistency.

7 Transfer to 6 serving plates and spoon the raspberry sauce over. Decorate with mint sprigs and reserved strawberries. Serve with cream.

chocolate zabaglione

serves four

4 egg yolks

4 tbsp superfine sugar

1¾ oz/50 g dark chocolate

½ cup Marsala wine

amaretti cookies, to serve

COOK'S TIP

Make the dessert just before serving as it will separate if you let it stand. If it begins to curdle, remove it from the heat immediately and put it into a bowl of cold water to stop the cooking. Whisk furiously until the mixture comes together.

1 In a large glass mixing bowl, using an electric whisk, whisk the egg yolks and superfine sugar together until you have a very pale mixture.

2 Grate the chocolate finely and fold into the egg mixture.

3 Fold the Marsala wine into the chocolate mixture.

4 Put the mixing bowl over a pan of gently simmering water and set the electric whisk on the lowest speed or change to a hand-held balloon whisk. Cook, whisking continuously until the mixture thickens; take care not to overcook or the mixture will curdle.

5 Spoon the hot mixture into 4 warmed glass dishes or large coffee cups. Serve the zabaglione as soon as possible so that it is warm, light, and fluffy accompanied by amaretti cookies.

zabaglione

serves four

5 egg yolks

½ cup superfine sugar

⅔ cup Marsala wine or sweet sherry

amaretti cookies, to serve (optional)

1 Put the egg yolks into a large
mixing bowl.

2 Add the superfine sugar to the
egg yolks and whisk until the
mixture is thick and very pale and has
doubled in volume.

3 Put the bowl containing the egg
yolk and sugar mixture over a pan
of simmering water.

4 Add the Marsala wine or sherry to
the egg yolk and sugar mixture
and continue whisking until the foam
mixture becomes warm. This process
may take as long as 10 minutes.

5 Pour the mixture, which should
be light and frothy, into 4 tall
wine glasses.

6 Serve the zabaglione warm with
amaretti cookies, if you wish.

quick tiramisù

serves four

1 cup mascarpone or full-fat
   soft cheese
1 egg, separated
2 tbsp natural yogurt
2 tbsp superfine sugar
2 tbsp dark rum
2 tbsp strong black coffee
8 lady-fingers
2 tbsp grated dark chocolate

1 Put the cheese into a large mixing bowl, add the egg yolk, and yogurt, and beat until smooth.

2 Put the egg white into a large, spotlessly clean grease-free bowl and whisk until stiff but not dry. Whisk in the sugar and carefully fold into the cheese mixture.

3 Spoon half of the mixture into 4 large sundae glasses.

4 Mix the rum and coffee together in a shallow dish. Dip the lady-fingers into the rum mixture. Break them in half, or into smaller pieces if necessary, and divide among the sundae glasses.

5 Stir any remaining coffee mixture into the remaining cheese and spoon over the top.

6 Sprinkle with grated chocolate. and serve or chill until required.

honey & nut nests

serves four

8 oz/225 g angel hair pasta

8 tbsp butter

1½ cups shelled pistachio
    nuts, chopped

½ cup sugar

⅓ cup honey

⅝ cup water

2 tsp lemon juice

salt

strained plain yogurt, to serve

COOK'S TIP

Angel hair pasta is also known
as capelli d'Angelo. Long and
very fine, it is usually sold in
small bunches that already
resemble nests.

---

1 Bring a large pan of lightly salted water to a boil over a medium heat. Add the pasta and cook until done. Drain the pasta thoroughly and return to the pan. Add the butter and, using 2 forks, toss to coat the pasta thoroughly. Let cool.

2 Arrange 4 small flan or poaching rings on a cookie sheet. Divide the pasta into 8 equal quantities and spoon 4 of them into the rings. Press down lightly. Top with half the nuts, then add the remaining pasta.

3 Cook in a preheated oven at 350°F/180°C, for 45 minutes, or until golden brown.

4 Meanwhile, put the sugar, honey, and water in a small pan and bring to a boil over a low heat, stirring continuously until the sugar has dissolved. Simmer for 10 minutes, then add the lemon juice and simmer for an additional 5 minutes.

5 Using a spatula, carefully transfer the angel hair nests to a serving dish. Pour over the honey syrup, then sprinkle over the remaining nuts and let cool completely before serving. Serve with the strained plain yogurt.